TRUE
WEALTH

ISBN: 9798388341631

Imprint: Independently published

Copyright 2022, Paul Tracey.

Provest Wealth Management is a trading name of Provest Financial Solutions LLP. Provest Financial Solutions LLP is a Limited Liability Partnership registered in England and Wales Number OC343605.

This book was produced in collaboration with Write Business Results Limited. For more information on their business book and marketing services, please visit www.writebusinessresults.com or contact the team via info@writebusinessresults.com.

TRUE WEALTH

Achieving Peace of Mind and Wellbeing With Financial Life Planning

PAUL TRACEY

With contributions from Simon Cartmell

ACKNOWLEDGEMENTS

The essence of this book is distilled from over three decades of studying, reading, attending conferences and seminars, and all that I have learned from some of the giants of financial services and personal development:

Andrew Dodson for his friendship, business coaching and leadership.

Paula Etheridge for the introduction to and training in professional financial planning.

Paul Armson and Mitch Anthony for inspiring and insightful teaching.

John Dashfield for being both a friend and a coach, and for introducing me to the three principles which have made a huge difference to my life.

Simon Cartmell for his enormous contribution to this book and the quality of his advice.

To Dan Sullivan and Strategic Coach® for providing the platform and strategic thinking tools that have taken our business to the next level.

To all the people that I've met within the various professional bodies: the LIA, PFS, the Institute of Financial Planning, and MDRT® where I first saw Bill Bachrach speak, which was a huge game changer for me in developing my understanding of how financial planning and advice should be delivered.

Georgia Kirke and her team at Write Business Results for their professionalism and guidance with this project and for making this book happen.

To all of our clients who have entrusted us with their financial wellbeing.

DEDICATION

My wife Liz for her love and her unwavering
support in life and business.

My children, Megan and Luke, for the joy and the
constant reminder of what really matters and what's
really important in life.

My mother Diane, for her strength and guidance and who was
instrumental in me starting my career in financial services.

To Richard for being a rock.

My brother Wayne and my sister Kerrie for the journey
we have had together and how we have grown.

To all my family and friends, many of whom have become
clients along the way – you are all really important to me.

And finally, to my team past and present, as I couldn't
do what I do without you.

FOREWORD

How do you think of wealth? I would guess that most of us tend to think of wealth in terms of money. The majority of financial advisers and advisory firms take this view too and work within that narrow definition of wealth.

Yet there is a rare but growing breed of financial adviser who understands that the true definition of wealth is much broader than being purely about the money. True wealth is, first and foremost, about living a high quality of life, not simply having an abundance of money or possessions. After all, what is the point of being financially wealthy if you are miserable, unhappy, and stressed out at the same time?

I first met Paul Tracey as a co-attendee on a business coaching programme back in the late 1990s. Back then I owned a financial advisory practice myself, which I went on to sell several years later. In the early 2000s I set up a business coaching practice of my own and have collaborated with many financial advisers, including some of the leading financial planning firms in the UK.

Upon meeting Paul, I immediately warmed to him and am proud to count him as a close friend. I see him as the epitome of this new breed of financial adviser. It also happens to be true that many other financial advisers are inspired by Paul too. They see him as a role model and seek his guidance, which he always generously gives.

Primarily, Paul is concerned with how you want to live your life. What matters most to you? Who matters most to you? What are your deepest held values? What does your life look like when living through these values? So, a conversation with Paul is enlightening because how often do any of us pause and reflect deeply on how we are living our precious lives? After a meeting with Paul, people experience a renewed sense of clarity about their lives and a new platform from which to make important life decisions.

It is only after gaining a thorough understanding of you and what you want from life that Paul will turn the attention to money. He understands that money is a means to an end and a tool to be used to live the life you want and make the difference that you want to make in the world.

This book is an extension of Paul's approach, making it available to you and applicable in your own life. I recommend that you grasp this opportunity with both hands and follow what Paul can teach you.

When you do this, you will find a renewed sense of clarity about your life and, most likely, a new and refreshing relationship with money.

John Dashfield

Dashfield Coaching & Development Ltd

PREFACE

While Paul is the author of this book, what you are about to read echoes the values, thoughts and ethos that his business, Provest Wealth Management, embodies. The information and guidance shared in the coming chapters is a product not only of Paul's journey, experience and rationale, but also that of the entire Provest team.

The Provest mission statement is a fitting way to start the book, and to give you a flavour of what's to come:

> At Provest we work as a team to improve the quality of life and provide peace of mind for those who seek our advice and commit to working with us.
>
> Our clients appreciate that they are the custodians of their wealth and its future benefit will be determined by successful planning. They may use it to achieve and maintain the lifestyle they want throughout their lives. If looked after well, this wealth can be a legacy

that they then gift to future generations or causes that are important to them, lasting long after they have passed and no longer need it themselves. We ensure this can be achieved in the most tax-efficient manner and that their beneficiaries are able to understand that they inherit not just the money, but the responsibility to continue as custodians themselves and plan accordingly. Money can be spent but true wealth can, and should, be passed on.

INTRODUCTION

This book is all about understanding the concept of real wealth and learning what true wealth means to you as an individual. The notion that wealth equates to how much you have in your bank account is one that is all too often peddled by the mainstream media, but how many people do you know with more money than they will ever need who feel unfulfilled and unhappy? Maybe you even fall into this camp. If so, don't worry, because this book will help you uncover what true wealth means to you and show you what steps you can take to move towards the future you want to live.

As you'll learn in the first part of this book, a happy life is one that is value driven, rather than one that is driven by accumulating ever-more money. I want to help you see that your earnings and your business are a vehicle for achieving your ideal life. They are a tool you can use to create a wealthy life and leave a legacy that will benefit your loved ones.

This might sound obvious when you see it written on the page, and you may even be wondering why you've never considered this before. The answer is, likely, time (or a lack thereof). As a business owner myself, I know all too well how easy it is to stay "in" your business. You love being busy, but you're constantly at risk of being overwhelmed by everything you need to do to keep your company performing and growing.

You may only be considering what you want to achieve in your life, beyond your business, for the first time. If you're reading this book, chances are that you have only engaged with financial planning at a superficial level to date. I'm here to help you step off the hamster wheel of your business and get a bird's-eye view of your life. There are many pieces that make up your "true wealth puzzle", but they aren't always easy to spot when you're stuck in the details.

I'm going to explore the three key areas that I believe we all need to consider to not only enjoy life in the present, but also to make sure we can enjoy our future and (hopefully) a long and fulfilling retirement. These areas are the past, present and future. I'd like you to think of each of these as a section of your true wealth jigsaw puzzle that comprises various important pieces. It's only when you get all the pieces in place that you can see the big picture – or in this case, live the fulfilled life you truly desire. This is real wealth.

In my decades of experience as a financial planner, I've noticed people often focus too heavily on their past and their present perceived reality, and they forget to plan effectively for their future. I'm all for living in the here and now, but while also keeping one eye on the future. I encourage my clients to do the same and to start framing their decisions, financial and otherwise, around how they will affect their future selves. However, it's important to understand your past and present to allow you to take effective steps towards the future you want to create.

Understanding your past

Financial advisers typically get a snapshot of the financial past and present of their clients and try to build a plan that will help to project the future. However, as they narrow their fact-finding process primarily to data gathering, clients may feel that their advisers know their numbers but don't know *them*. It is important that you and any financial adviser you work with understands your roots and values, as well as what the connections are between who, what or where is important to you.

There are several questions that can prove illuminating. For example, exploring some of the best financial decisions you've made in the past will reveal your financial knowledge and understanding of risk, and might also reveal mistakes and shortcomings.

Being able to explain how you accumulated what you have today will reveal financial disciplines (or a lack thereof) and may indicate the need for structured saving programmes. Did you build your assets through a disciplined process or a fortunate circumstance?

What lessons you learnt about money when you were growing up will reveal values regarding money, any levels of financial instruction you've received and your relationship with money, including whether this is conflicting or harmonious.

You and your advisers need to understand how you got to where you are today in terms of your life's work and how you started your business, as this will reveal the goals, directions and course that you may have taken, possibly also uncovering work satisfaction or business ambitions.

One final question to consider is whether you have ever known anyone who has lived a very fulfilling life or possibly retired successfully and what contributed to that success. Exploring the answer to this question might reveal your vision – or lack thereof – and whether you have a realistic picture of what will help to maintain a contented life.

Exploring your present situation

Establishing what's happening right now is the next important step for creating a financial plan and helping you move towards a fulfilled life. You need to consider what's happening with your family, other people's needs that will be affected by the financial decisions you make, and for whom you feel a sense of financial responsibility.

Understanding the most important thing that money gives you today reveals your values and priorities, and helps you to determine what money represents in your life. Additionally, the concerns and fears that you have might affect the financial decisions that you make. It's also essential to explore what life transitions you and your family are presently going through, as these may need to be addressed at a transactional or educational level.

As I asked earlier, if you had all the money in the world what would you do differently? The answer you give to this question will help to reveal how happy you are with your current life or work situation, establish what is really important to you, as well as highlight any possibly unrealistic expectations you have about what money can do for you.

When it comes to investing money, you also have to ask whether you have any principles that will affect your decisions in line with social responsibility and your overall values. Also, pay attention to where you look for information regarding money and finances and how this influences you in your decision-making around money.

Identifying your future plans

Looking to the future, a good question to start with is: how would you like to change your lifestyle going forward, if at all? This will reveal the lifestyle that you currently desire.

The next thing to consider is what you would do in your work or business life if it was really up to you, as this will reveal your thinking about what motivates you to spend more time "doing" while you're at work. Also think about what might give you the best results from the time and effort that you put into your business and work life.

It is also important to explore your biggest concerns about your financial future and getting older, as this may reveal the issues that you're worrying about. Once you know what these are, look at whether these are issues you can affect as they are in your control – such as your business, personal relationships or health – or not affect as they are out of your control, such as the economy and world political affairs.

You might also want to consider what you're most looking forward to both in the short and long term as you transition to different stages of your life, including retirement.

Being able to paint a picture of what future financial independence looks like for you is also important. Does it provide you with the freedom of time and the freedom of the people that you spend time with? Will you have purpose in your life and what will you do with your time?

How you want to spend your time is an especially important consideration for the future, particularly what you would like to do for or with your partner, spouse, family, children or grandchildren. You also have to think about practicalities, such as what you would like to do with your property and whether you will be able to manage it as you get older. You can also make a list of what you would like to do, see or experience and with whom, as well as what it might cost.

Ask yourself whether you have enough time currently to do the things that are important to you and, if the answer is no, what are you going to do differently, going forward?

Personal growth is very important to give us purpose. So, what would you like to learn or what hobbies would you like to spend more time doing? What new skills would you like to study or develop and are there any financial costs to these?

In my experience nearly every client wants to spend more time travelling and experiencing more of the world and its different cultures, so where would you like to travel and what would you like to see whilst you're there? This will affect the financial decisions you make to either go and experience these now if you already have enough, or to ensure that you're making provisions to allow you to do this later in your life but whilst you're still fit and able to do so.

It's also good to decide the top ten things that you want to do whilst you still can. What are your dreams and fantasies, and what adventures are you looking forward to? Perhaps a more important question is what have you been putting off that will motivate you to plan and take action with this list?

Finally, you need to consider potential changes in circumstances, such as the life transitions you may see in the next five years or even over the longer term that you need to prepare for right now. Thinking about these will help establish what financial planning is necessary going forward.

These transitions might be providing education funding for your children or grandchildren, getting married or even divorced, starting a new job, or a new business or even exiting the business through a sale. It could also involve dealing with the health of elderly parents and other close family members.

These are all examples of life transitions that will have a major impact on your overall life and financial wellbeing, particularly if you do not prepare for them today.

Roald Amundsen: the benefits of having all the pieces of the puzzle

"Victory awaits him who has everything in order – luck, people call it. Defeat is certain for him who has neglected to take the necessary precautions in time; this is called bad luck."

Roald Amundsen

You are more than likely aware of Roald Amundsen as a historical figure. For many in Britain, he is simply the polar explorer who beat Robert Falcon Scott to the South Pole in 1911; his role merely a "bit part" in the tragic story of Scott and his ill-fated expedition. But Amundsen is a case study in what can happen when you have all the pieces of your puzzle in order; and when you have considered the past, the present and the future.

The expedition

Both Scott and Amundsen set out on their ambitious expeditions to reach the South Pole at the end of 1911, as the Antarctic winter was waning. Both teams encountered temperatures of -50 degrees C. As you no doubt know, Amundsen not only reached the South Pole first, but also made it back safely, with all of his team alive.

Scott, on the other hand, made it to the South Pole only to discover the Norwegian flag of Amundsen's team already planted in the snow. Scott and his entire party perished on their return journey. One of the most tragic elements of their story is that they were less than a day away from their next supply depot when they succumbed to starvation and the cold. So, how did Amundsen succeed while Scott failed? The answers lie in Amundsen's approach that encompassed the past, present and future.

The past

Amundsen and his team spent months training with the indigenous people of the Arctic to learn vital survival skills and prepare themselves for the conditions they would encounter in the South Pole. Unlike Scott's expedition, which relied on motorised sleds, all of which broke down due to the freezing conditions, Amundsen stuck with the tried-and-tested method of huskies pulling sleds. He took 52 dogs on the expedition with his team of five men.

The present

Amundsen planned with productive paranoia for everything that could go wrong during the expedition. His team took three tons of food for his expedition, which meant they could afford to miss a couple of their supply depot stops. Scott had 17 men on his team and only took one ton of food for the trip, which meant they could not afford to miss even a single supply depot.

Amundsen also took four thermometers, in case any should break, while Scott had only one (which did break). This left Scott's team unaware of, and therefore vulnerable to, rapid falls in temperature.

On the journey itself, Amundsen and his team were incredibly disciplined, travelling 15 to 20 miles each day, regardless of the weather conditions. He had calculated the distance they needed to cover to get to and from the pole safely, and his intention was to ensure his team rested throughout the journey. His discipline paid off, as he reached the South Pole on 14 December 1911, having averaged 15.5 miles per day.

Amundsen's team also safely made their return journey, arriving back at their ship on 25 January 1912, five days ahead of schedule.

Of course, the tragic outcome for Scott's team is well-known. Although they successfully reached the South Pole on 17 January 1912, they all perished on their return journey. Unlike Amundsen, who had travelled a consistent distance each day whether conditions were good or poor, Scott had chosen to travel as far as 45 miles on days when conditions were favourable, but to bunker down and not gain a single mile on days when they were poor.

The future

Amundsen's productive paranoia for the things that could go wrong, as well as his time spent with the Inuit, allowed him to plan effectively for both the outward and return journeys. One of the steps he took to future-proof the expedition was to place black stones in circles up to one kilometre around each of their supply depots, thereby ensuring they would still find them even if they became covered in snow or the team veered slightly off course.

Amundsen and his team didn't miss a single supply depot on their journey. Scott and his team were tragically within reach of one when they all died on their return from the South Pole, because they couldn't see it due to the snow that had blown over and covered it.

Before Amundsen set out on his expedition, he had a plan that was crystal clear. He had considered every eventuality he could, made provisions for the worst while hoping for the best, and as a result not only arrived at the South Pole on the very day he planned to, but ended up completing the return journey early. He had a clear vision of his future in mind (the successful expedition to the South Pole) and he took all the necessary steps to execute it, including finding a landing point for his ship that shaved 60 miles off his journey compared to Scott's chosen route.

While Scott's story is undoubtedly tragic, when you compare the two expeditions you can see that he didn't carry out the same degree of preparation or planning as Amundsen and that, as a result, both he and his team paid the ultimate price.

Amundsen not only collected all the pieces of his puzzle, but he put them together and studied the bigger picture before setting off, all of which made the difference to the outcome he experienced.[1]

1   Details from a presentation given by Robert Gardner in 2012 (then co-founder of Redington)

Piecing together your true wealth jigsaw puzzle

It can help to think of your future life as a jigsaw puzzle that is composed of pieces you've already collected in your past, pieces you have now in your present, and pieces you'll need in the future to complete the picture you're creating. When you are able to put all of these together in the right order, you can piece together a truly wealthy future, where you are living a content and fulfilled life and where your loved ones are taken care of, in some cases for generations to come.

However, the challenge for most people is that they haven't ever examined the pieces they've collected to see what's missing from their puzzle, and nor have they ever taken the time to work out what the completed puzzle should look like.

When you start putting together a jigsaw puzzle, you look at the picture on the box to help you determine where it's best to start. If you can't see that picture, you're likely to find the whole process much more challenging. This is where a financial planner can be invaluable. I help my clients work out what their picture looks like, I examine the various pieces of the puzzle that they already have and I help fill in the gaps, or advise them about how they can find the missing pieces themselves.

As you read the chapters in this book, my hope is that you'll find different pieces of your puzzle and take your first steps towards considering what your picture looks like.

Take a holistic approach to your financial future

Depending on your experience of financial advice and financial planning to date, you may believe the outdated narrative that this is all about money. This is far from true. My aim with every client is to take a holistic approach to building their financial future, but the foundations for this are understanding each person's values, purpose, goals and what legacy they want to leave. Only once these four pillars are in place do we talk about money.

Many business owners set out to achieve a lifestyle that enables them plenty of freedom. Sadly, many find the opposite and become trapped on a hamster wheel, constantly trying to accumulate more money in the belief that this is what they need to do. What I'd like to do through this book is get you to pause and consider your situation. If money was no object, what would your life look like right now?

One of the concepts I'll explore in Part 1 of this book is that of behavioural finance. It's important to examine our habits and behaviours surrounding our finances, because these are not always helpful and, by changing some of the negative habits and behaviours into positive ones, you can make a big stride towards achieving the fulfilled, wealthy life you desire.

Taking the time to focus on yourself

As a business owner, I know all too well how easy it can be to put your own wellbeing on the back burner as you work to manage and grow a thriving company. However, failing to spend time on your own development not only harms you, but also your business in the long term.

Working closely with a financial planner, as you will learn, is time well spent and, indeed, will often save you time and effort in the years to come. In fact, once you have created a comprehensive financial life plan, you may only require one high-quality meeting a year to assess progress and any changes in circumstances, including current life events, and then to adjust it to keep you on track for the future you want. Surely that's worth the time and effort?

Before I get into the specifics of how a financial planner can support you on this journey, I'd like to start by inviting you to think about your own beliefs around money, where those come from and whether there are any that you would benefit from updating. Let's get started by taking a look at your past and where your beliefs around money stem from.

Part 1:

YOUR REALITY OF THE PAST

In this first part of the book, I'm going to look at where some of our beliefs around money come from – from a societal perspective – and I invite you to start exploring your own money beliefs. These are often passed onto us by parents and influential people in our lives. In many cases, we are not consciously aware of them until we take the time to question our financial decision making and why we have made certain choices throughout our lives.

This is why the concept of behavioural finance – which I'll talk about in detail in Chapter 2 – is so important, because it encourages us to look at what is driving our behaviour around our money and to decide whether our behaviour will help or hinder us to achieve our goals and the life we desire.

It's also important at this stage to look at the term "wealth" and what it really means. Does living a wealthy life mean you have millions in the bank? Or can someone with considerably less money still lead a very wealthy life? I certainly believe the latter, but take the time to check in with yourself here and think about how you view wealth.

Identifying your values, what's important to you in life and what lifestyle you would like to lead are equally important at this stage. These are some of the most foundational pieces of your metaphorical puzzle and as you uncover each one, you will gain much greater clarity over both where you want to head in the future, and why you are in your current situation.

It's also important to note that not all beliefs about money are negative and, indeed, you may have some very positive financial beliefs and behaviours that have helped you get to where you are today, and that will continue to serve you well in the future. However, without consciously examining your beliefs and behaviour, you won't know this for certain.

Certainty is one of the biggest and most important puzzle pieces when it comes to leading a content and fulfilled life, and the only way to achieve certainty is to spread all the pieces out on the table, examine each in turn and use this as an opportunity to learn about yourself at a deeper level.

Chapter 1

WHAT DOES "TRUE WEALTH" MEAN TO YOU?

Money can't buy you happiness...

Money can't buy you happiness is a common phrase we have all heard thrown around, but there is growing evidence that this is the case. John Caudwell, founder of Phones4U, is a case in point. He has even been open about the fact that his vast wealth doesn't shield him from unhappiness or challenges in his life.

In a 2015 interview[2], the philanthropist and businessman, who at the time was worth an estimated £2 billion, said that there are some days when he only registers a score of just one or two

2   Stanford P., (2015), 'The unhappy billionaire: 'I have billions - but massive sadness in my life, too', *Stuff*, 8 September, available at: https://www.stuff.co.nz/life-style/well-good/71815484/the-unhappy-billionaire-i-have-billions---but-massive-sadness-in-my-life-too

on the happiness scale, even though he feels as if he should be a "nine or ten".

"If you think having money means that life is going to be fantastic all the time, that you can move from one wonderful thing to the next even more wonderful thing, then you need to recalibrate," Caudwell told BBC show, *Britain's Spending Secrets.*

He revealed that his oldest son, Rufus, has been diagnosed with Lyme disease. Although the bacterial infection is relatively easy to treat with antibiotics if it is caught in its early stages, it is also incredibly hard to diagnose and early symptoms are often mistaken for other conditions. This is what happened in Rufus' case.

Although Caudwell is financially supporting a team of people researching Lyme disease and the specialist treatment Rufus requires, he describes his son's health problems as "a massive sadness in my life".

He believes that it's possible for billionaires to be happy, if that's what they want to achieve, but he is also adamant that it's just as possible to be happy if you're penniless. In fact, this is one of the lessons he has passed onto his five children. The other is advice we could all stand to live by: "However much money you have, you should try to leave the world a better place."

Interestingly, Caudwell also said that he feels he has had time to "acclimatise" to his wealth, because he built it up over the course of 40 years through his business.

His experiences are also supported by Clay Cockrell, a psychotherapist who has many ultra-high- net-worth individuals as his clients. In an article for *The Guardian*[3], Cockrell revealed that many of his clients are "bored with life" and struggle to find a reason to get out of bed each day. They have no purpose to guide them. Many are also suspicious of new people who enter their lives, constantly questioning what that person wants from them, or wondering how they will try to manipulate them.

It's a lonely place to be. Cockrell also feels many of his incredibly wealthy clients have over-indulged their children and failed to prepare them for the realities of managing the wealth they will one day inherit, or even to talk to them about money and basic financial skills at all. "It can be very difficult to watch these individuals struggle with the toxicity of excess, isolation and deep mistrust," Cockrell writes.

---

3   Cockrell C., (2021), 'I'm a therapist to the super-rich: they are as miserable as Succession makes out', *The Guardian*, 22 November, available at: https://www.theguardian.com/commentisfree/2021/nov/22/therapist-super-rich-succession-billionaires?CMP=share_btn_link

It would seem the old adage is true, money truly can't buy you happiness.

What does the word "wealth" mean to you? In my experience there is a common misconception that wealth relates solely to money. That's entirely understandable, given that the financial services industry got hold of the word and has been using it in relation to money for decades. However, the word "wealth" actually comes from the word "weal" that means "wellbeing". This, in turn, stemmed from the Old English word for wellbeing: "wela"[4].

So, as you can see the original meaning of the word "wealth" is much broader than money and encompasses our wellbeing, even though it has now become so narrowly defined by many in our society. It's not only the origins of the word that point to its true meaning; you can find examples in the Bible where wealth is used as a term to determine someone's quality of life, rather than the amount of money they have.

If you have always considered wealth with reference to your money and physical possessions, consider this a point at which you can check in and start to see the world a little differently. I

---

4   Merriam-Webster Dictionary definition, viewed on 25/1/2022, available at: https://www.merriam-webster.com/dictionary/weal

view money as a tool to be used to support and enhance your wellbeing and to enable you to live a happy and fulfilled life. There is one magic word you can use that will help you start to unpick your perception of wealth relating to money: why.

If your goal at this moment in time is to be rich, I would invite you to ask yourself why you want to be rich. Is it so you can own a particular car, buy a bigger house, go on nice holidays? What happens when you achieve that goal? Will you be happy and fulfilled? In my experience, chasing money and possessions alone does not lead to a happy or fulfilled life. However, when you start to think about how you can use money as a vehicle to get you what you want, you start to make progress towards that happy and fulfilled life. When you view money as a tool, you start to use your money in the right way and make smart decisions with it that will help you achieve what you truly want. Usually this isn't a bigger bank balance but peace of mind and freedom of choice. It's a much more comprehensive view of your wellbeing.

In my experience, if you see money as the solution you will typically find it becomes the problem. When you chase a figure, it gradually drives discontent with your life. I remember when I first started working when I was around 18–19 years old, I thought £10,000 a year would be enough. Suddenly, you realise that isn't going to be enough, so you start aiming to earn

£30,000 a year... Then £50,000 a year... It's a never-ending cycle, the figure is always moving. This is why if you focus solely on a monetary goal, you will generally find that contentment and happiness is elusive in your life.

All too often, the likes of quality of life, working time and happiness get discussed adjacent to wealth, but I believe these are at the heart of true wealth, rather than elements that are simply adjacent to the concept of having a wealthy life. Uncovering what "wealthy" looks like for you involves digging into your why and getting clear on what you will use your money for.

When you take the time to explore your why, you are taking a step back and thinking about what will really make you happy. It can be very easy to tell ourselves that a new car/holiday abroad/ bigger house (there are many more I could add) will make us happy, but we rarely stop to evaluate whether that is actually true. When you understand what true wealth means to you, it's empowering because it puts you in a position to make a truly informed choice about how you live your life.

This gives you a chance to reprioritise and ensure that your focus truly is on leading a life that makes you happy and fulfilled, rather than chasing the next "shiny thing" in the hope that this will make you happy. Instead you will know what will make you happy and what will enable you to live a fulfilled life.

In my experience, once people gain clarity about their why it turns out that it is very rarely about money in the bank but about the peace of mind that their money gives them. Most people want to know that they're going to be comfortable, can maintain the lifestyle they're accustomed to and can have the experiences they want in life. This can be incredibly valuable when there are concerns about the rising cost of living, because knowing that you won't have to struggle financially alleviates a great deal of stress and anxiety.

My aim is to give each and every one of my clients real peace of mind that not only will they be OK financially, but that they can also live life on their terms, in line with what's important whilst enjoying the experiences that mean the most to them.

What's your Return on Life™?

Return on Life™ is a concept that was developed by US-based financial planning coach and author Mitch Anthony. This is a concept that I use with my clients and one that is incredibly powerful. The basic premise is simple: it's about looking at the return you get on your life beyond anything financial.

Imagine you're reviewing your financial position in 20 years' time. You've accumulated more money than you could ever need and you've received an annual return of nine per cent on your money, but you haven't got round to doing everything you wanted to do. You've had a totally unbalanced life.

Now imagine that you could give up two per cent of that return and achieve more of what you wanted to do in your life. Would you sacrifice that percentage of your money for a more balanced and fulfilled life? When I pose this question to clients, often the response is a resounding "Yes!". This is all about focusing on what really matters to you and what you want to do with the rest of your life. Once we know this, we can organise your money around those objectives, rather than money being a goal in and of itself.

I'm sure you know people who, despite having very little financial wealth, are incredibly happy in their lives. On the other side, you will no doubt know of people with millions in the bank who are just not happy. Wealth itself cannot be translated solely into monetary terms, otherwise it would be replicable and we would have a physical target where we could say, "If I have below X level I'm miserable, at Y level I'm okay and when I get above Z level I'm going to be deliriously happy." We all know that money and life aren't like that.

What I am talking about is understanding what motivates you. If money doesn't matter to you, that's fine, as long as you can achieve the lifestyle that you want with what you have. The level of money you need is very personal and it's different for everyone. If we're honest, the majority of people don't want a superyacht, a private aeroplane or whatever else the media might class as being part of a "wealthy" life; they simply want to know that they can continue to live in the manner they've become accustomed to without having to worry about what the future holds. Money is a means to an end.

By the end of this book, I hope that you will not only understand what true wealth means to you, but that you will be in a position to build a plan to enable you to achieve this level of satisfaction with your life.

Finding your place on the money scale

A report released by the Office for National Statistics in January 2022, revealed that the wealthiest ten per cent of households held 43 per cent of all the wealth in Great Britain in the latest period (April 2018 to March 2020); in comparison, the bottom 50 per cent held only nine per cent. The richest one per cent of households were those whose total wealth was more than £3.6

million. The least wealthy ten per cent of households had wealth of £15,400 or less[5].

Figure 2: The richest 1% of households had wealth of more than £3.6 million, least wealthy 10% had £15,400 or less

Household total wealth by percentiles, Great Britain, April 2018 to March 2020

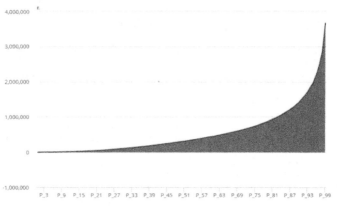

Source: The Office for National Statistics - Wealth and Assets Survey

5   Office for National Statistics, 7 January 2022, "Household total wealth in Great Britain: April 2018 to March 2020', available at: https://www.ons.gov.uk/peoplepopulationandcommunity/personalandhouseholdfinances/incomeandwealth/bulletins/totalwealthingreatbritain/april2018tomarch2020#

34

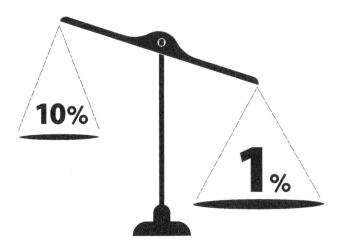

If you think about levels of wealth in terms of a scale, where you have the megarich at one end and people living in poverty on the other, would you know where on that scale you sit? There are two diametrically opposed worlds on this scale and there are people at both extremes living in the same country. The reality for most of us is that we're closer to the bottom end of the scale than we are to the top. Just take a moment now to think about where you would sit.

However, when you think about wealth and how it has been distributed in the past, you can see that we are probably wealthier than we've ever been as a society, yet despite this, there is a real unhappiness in many people. What I've observed is that this wealth doesn't buy people any real happiness if they don't have an understanding of what they want to achieve with it.

In the past, money was a necessity and provided a vehicle whereby you could exchange goods and services. However, we have shifted to a time when we spend money for the pleasure of it, in some cases, without any consideration for the future. The result is that, potentially for the first time ever, future generations will be worse off than the previous generation. By writing this book, I want to help educate current and future generations about how to lead wealthy lives and see money as a tool to achieve your goals, rather than a goal itself.

As my colleague Simon Cartmell observes: "Now we have a better life expectancy, quality of life and standard of living than before. This has grown so exponentially in the last 40 years that when you look back at what life was like in the 1970s and '80s, it's a completely alien world. Younger people today find this shift particularly hard to grasp, especially because technology is continuing to evolve so rapidly."

Have we lost our way?

When you look at the history of money, you can see that it started as a necessity to enable us to fulfil the foundational levels of the pyramid in Maslow's Hierarchy of Needs. We needed money to have shelter, feed ourselves and put clothes on our backs. While this is still true, we have somehow reached a point where money has become something that has the potential to make you happy.

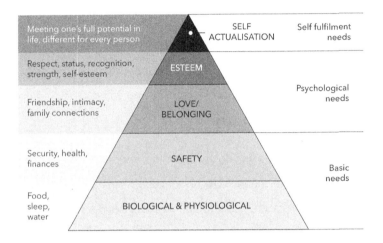

This is where we have lost our way, because we have been fed this idea that money brings happiness and that spending money brings pleasure. This world of consumerism that we've lived in since the 1990s has been built on the premise that if you own this or buy that, you will be happy. It's the story we're sold by advertisers in every industry. However, the truth is that money alone doesn't make you happy. It's just one piece of your wealth puzzle, albeit an important one.

Breaking the cycle

This cycle of chasing money in the belief it will lead to happiness can be broken by changing your thinking about money. To change your thinking, you have to begin by understanding what it is, because your thinking will be your reality. Your thinking stems from your beliefs, many of which you will have picked up unconsciously throughout your life.

What I want to help you do over the course of the coming chapters is to create new, higher quality beliefs around money and I'll do this by encouraging you to ask better questions. Once you get your thinking around money right, you'll be in a position where you can set out a roadmap to help you organise your money that is based upon your thinking, your values and what is truly important to you.

Of course, to do this you need to first identify what is truly important to you and then take control of it. Humans are known for telling stories, so the question to ask is, who is telling your story if it's not you? Are you living someone else's financial story if you aren't writing your own? I want to help you control your own narrative, because when you do this, you control your future and this means you can achieve the new objectives you set out for your life.

Where do your finances fall into this picture? If you know your finances are taken care of for the coming days, weeks, months and even the next year, this gives you the security to explore what is truly important to you and to set goals that will allow you to achieve what you want from your life. What you want to achieve will be personal; we all have different goals. When you organise your finances and have the knowledge that your future is secure, you will realise you have independence, choice and freedom, which in turn empowers you to steer your life in the direction you want.

This feeds back into the concept of Maslow's Hierarchy of Needs, in that, for the vast majority of us to be able to focus on the upper levels of that pyramid, we need to have our basic needs taken care of and secured.

What's your vision of the future?

To create a strong vision for what you want to do with the rest of your life, what's really important to you and how you will live that life in line with your values, you need to examine your past, understand your present and then plan for the future.

You have to create a plan to help you reach this future, using money as a resource to get you there, rather than seeing it as the be-all and end-all. Since the onset of the Covid-19 pandemic, many more clients have told me that they value life experiences far more than material possessions. For all the challenges that the pandemic has presented, it has also given all of us an opportunity to evaluate and get clarity about what's important to us. From there, it's my role to help you work out how much is enough and how you can organise and make smart decisions about your money to help you create and follow your plan to the future you want, as well as to review it at appropriate intervals. It really is that simple – although that doesn't mean it's easy!

In the past, thinking around scarcity and insecurity drove certain habits, with some people deciding not to give something up today in order to prepare for tomorrow. However, there is a growing understanding and awareness that we need to have one eye on the future, because even though we can't predict what's around the corner or know how many years we have ahead of us, we understand that we have a limited time during which to experience life to the full and to lay down strong financial foundations that will support our future.

This isn't only about preparing financially for the future though, but also about identifying what you value and are therefore prepared to spend money on. For example, I spend money every month on a gym membership and a personal trainer to make sure that this aspect of my life is prioritised to the right level. The reason I do this is because my father had a stroke at the age of 39 and has been paralysed down one side ever since. He was a self-employed builder but he never worked again after his stroke. He has been supported on state benefits for 37 years now and, although he doesn't live a life of luxury, he is happier than many other people I know who have a lot more.

This experience of seeing my father having to learn to live with his disability after his stroke taught me that I should partially use my money firstly to enjoy what life has to offer and, just as importantly, to look after my health and do what I can to prevent something similar happening to me.

What are you striving for?

In the past, the goal for many people might have been to build a pile of money. The media tells us to build a pile of money because then we'll be happy. However, the reality is that you need to build a plan first, and then build a pile of money that allows you to deliver that plan.

Remember that too much money can make you just as miserable as too little money. Having too much stuff can make you miserable, just as having too little stuff can make you miserable. Money is not the cure, it's a placebo.

In this age of social media, we have an unprecedented opportunity to view other people's lives, albeit through a filtered window of what they want us to see. This can lead to feelings of envy and see us constantly comparing ourselves (often unfavourably) with others. This presents a danger that we could end up living a very inauthentic life because we are striving for something that someone else has, without stopping to think about whether that is what we truly want for ourselves.

As a financial planner I consider myself to be in a very privileged position because I get to have meaningful conversations with people where I help them ask those questions of themselves and understand what truly matters to them. To me, true wealth is living your life in line with your values and what's important to you, and organising your finances around this so that they support your values and what you consider to be important.

Exercise: Uncovering your values

There are three questions from George Kinder, Founder of the Kinder Institute of Life Planning, that I like to run through with my clients:

1. Imagine that you have all the money in the world; you've got pockets so deep you're never going to run out. You're free to

do whatever you want, so what would you do, experience or have if money was no object?

2. Now imagine that you've been to see the doctor and they've told you that you have five years left to live. You'll be fit and healthy during that period, but you only have five years left. What would you do? Who would you see? What would you experience?

3. Finally, imagine you've gone back to the doctor who tells you they made a mistake and that you only have a few days left to live. What would you wish that you had been, had or done?

Make a note of your answers; these will start to show you where your values lie if you weren't sure before.

Bronnie Ware, a palliative care nurse, wrote a book *The Top Five Regrets of the Dying*[6] based on what her patients told her as they neared the end of their lives. None of these regrets relate to wanting more money, but they do include wishing they had lived a life that was true to themselves, wishing they had spent less time working and wishing they had been more courageous in expressing their feelings.

---

6   Bronnie Ware, (2019), *The Top Five Regrets of the Dying: A Life Transformed by the Dearly Departing*, Hay House UK, second edition

Think of the exercise I've just shared as an opportunity to take stock of where you are in your life. In addition to the three questions above, honestly assess whether you're happy where you are, whether you know where you want to be and what changes you might need to make. If you don't have that level of clarity over your life, don't worry, as this is what this book is here to help with.

Sometimes, just removing yourself one step and looking at the bigger picture of your life can help you see where you are, where you want to be and, most importantly, how to plot a course from one to the other. This is all about working out what is necessary for you to live a fulfilled life. If that means you only need a two per cent return on your capital, don't introduce unnecessary stress and challenge by striving for a seven per cent return. Open your mind to the possibilities before you. Instead of fixating on the return you could get for your money, ask instead, "What will make me happy and what do I need to achieve that?"

Collecting the pieces of your True Wealth Puzzle

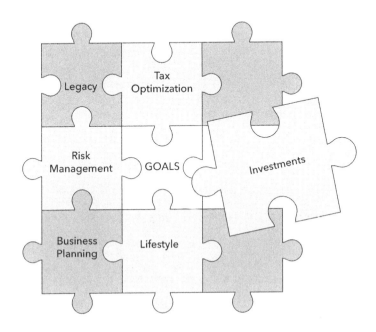

There are a number of tools that you can use to identify imbalance in your life and help you work out how close you are to (or how far away from) living an abundant life. Ultimately, the point of any of these tools is to encourage you to give a true and honest measurement of how you're performing in different areas of your life to start an internal dialogue about what you need to focus on and how you need to shift your priorities.

Among the areas that you usually assess as part of this kind of exercise is your health, finances, family, personal development, lifestyle (including your hobbies), work, relationships and purpose. There are other areas that you might consider important and also want to assess as part of building a fulfilled and truly wealthy life, such as philanthropy, social conscience and environmental impact. Which pieces you want to fit into your True Wealth Puzzle is up to you.

What you are looking for with each piece of your puzzle is that they are roughly the same size and therefore that they'll all click together. If you have one or two areas with a high score (let's say nine out of ten) and one or two that you're neglecting and give a score of four or five out of ten, you won't be able to put your puzzle together.

When you realise that there is an imbalance, the next step is to look at what needs to change in order to bring that balance into your life and ensure that all your puzzle pieces are the same size. So, if family is one of your priorities, but you're working 70 hours a week in your business and aren't spending time with your partner and children, your family puzzle piece will be considerably smaller than your work puzzle piece and the two won't click.

Realising that this is the case gives you an opportunity to assess what will need to change in your work life in order to increase the amount of time you're spending with your family. If you own your business, it could involve making it run more efficiently to allow you to step out a little more.

There are certain pieces of your True Wealth Puzzle that will be important regardless of your other priorities: your health, your finances and how you spend your time. Without your health, it can be difficult to fit other pieces of your puzzle together – what good is driving a Bentley if you can't get in or out of it?! As I've explained, your finances underpin your life but money is a tool to enable you to bring all the pieces of your puzzle into balance. On its own, it's no use, so your score for your financial situation needs to factor in how you are using your money to live a purposeful, fulfilled and happy life.

Time is the one resource in life that none of us can get back once we've spent it, so it's important to look at which pieces of your True Wealth Puzzle you are spending the most time on and to ensure that those are aligned with your values and help you create a balanced, happy and fulfilled life, whatever they may be.

So, the first thing to do is decide what pieces make up your True Wealth Puzzle, and from there you need to make sure that all of these pieces are of a similar size and that they can therefore fit together to create the life you want to live.

What does success mean to you?

It's important to not only understand what is important to you, but also to have some kind of metric so that you know when you are successful. Becoming clear about what success looks like to you will also help bring greater clarity to what's important for you in your life, because the two naturally feed into one another.

If you ask yourself this question in the context of having a plan that runs for maybe 10 or 15 years, think about what you would like to have achieved in that time. What do you want to happen by the end of that period of time? What would you consider to be a failure? There are no right or wrong answers to these questions, because they are highly subjective. What brings peace of mind for you might be entirely different from what brings peace of mind for someone else.

As well as identifying what success looks like, you have to commit to achieving that success. Having a plan is one thing, taking the actions necessary to achieve it are another. This is why it's essential that you're honest about what success really looks like for you, because this will help motivate you to work towards that end goal.

For example, let's say that I told you I wanted to run the London Marathon next year, raise £50,000 for charity in the process and complete it in sub-three hours. If I want to achieve any of those goals, I have to take the initial step of registering for a place to run the marathon; I will need to start training for it and I will need to fundraise. If I wait until the month before the marathon to take any of those steps, I'm setting myself up for failure. It might have been a flippant, throwaway comment, in which case I am unlikely to commit to what's required to achieve any of those goals.

If, on the other hand, I am fully committed to running the London Marathon in sub-three hours and raising all that money for charity because it's something I will find fulfilling, then I will be prepared to take those steps and, more than likely, to seek support along the way.

The key in either scenario is admitting what's truly important to you. If it's not important, you can let the idea go. It's really no different when it comes to putting together a financial plan. It really helps to work with an adviser who you can be completely open and honest with, as this will allow you to admit whether the goals you have are really what's important to you.

In my line of work, people typically come to me because they have a problem rather than simply because they are seeking peace of mind. However, by diving into the nuts and bolts of why something is a problem and what solving that problem means for them, I'm able to help them create a more robust and aligned plan for their finances and their future.

This requires a commitment on your side and some work to achieve the outcomes you want to see. However, this work doesn't have to be laborious or difficult. When you have the right support from your adviser, you can find the most suitable path to follow to achieve your goals and live a more fulfilled life.

Daniel and Helen: sharing the wealth

Daniel and Helen came to my firm because they wanted their money to work harder for them to enable them to do good things with it. They had been lucky enough to acquire wealth and they wanted to be philanthropic with it.

They had very little desire for money themselves; their focus was on what that money could do for others. We created an ethical solution and explored how this could give them the means to support their local church and charities they felt were important. The underlying aim was to give them a sustained ability to pass on their good fortune throughout the rest of their lives.

After carefully considering our plan, Daniel and Helen told us they had chosen to take a different path. "We've decided to give all the money to the church, and we'll let them decide how best to use it," they told us. We wished them well and fully respected their decision, because it was what truly made them satisfied. Our role was to guide Daniel and Helen and to make sure they had enough information to make an informed decision, even if what they decided wasn't what we were advising.

A piece of the puzzle

Understanding that money is not the goal, but a means to help you achieve your goals, is a very important mindset shift that can make a significant difference to your relationship with money and therefore the way in which you behave with money.

The concept of behavioural finance is particularly key to this, and one that I'll come back to in the next chapter. Very briefly, behavioural finance is about your financial decision making and what drives you to make certain decisions. Your perceptions and beliefs about money will be one of those drivers, which is why it's good to start by checking in with what your beliefs about money are and where those stem from. This is an important part of your wealth puzzle.

Knowing what you want to achieve and what will make you feel fulfilled and happy in life is another essential piece of the puzzle when it comes to creating a financial plan that you will follow through on. When the actions you have to take are deeply aligned to your goals in life, you are much more likely to do what's necessary.

Examining your various goals and ideas is a good exercise, because it can help you see which ones you are truly passionate about, and which you can let fall by the wayside. Wealth, as we already know, is not about how much money you have in the bank. It is about how you use what you have to lead the life you truly desire, whether that's giving away a sizable portion of your financial wealth to causes you are passionate about, providing for the next generation of your family or retiring at 50 and travelling the world.

In the next chapter, we're going to look at behavioural finance and why understanding this concept can be so beneficial for your financial and broader wellbeing, thereby helping you to grow and protect the wealth you have in your life.

Chapter 2

BEHAVIOURAL FINANCE

At its core, behavioural finance is about how people make financial decisions and what influences them to make those decisions. But why is behavioural finance important?

The main reason is that by showing how, when and why behaviour deviates from rational expectations, behavioural finance provides a blueprint that can help you make better, more logical decisions when it comes to your finances.

Behavioural finance encompasses five main behaviours:

- **Mental accounting:** This refers to the propensity for people to allocate money for specific purposes.

- **Herd behaviour:** Herd behaviour states that people tend to mimic the financial behaviours of the majority. Herding is notorious in the stock market as the cause behind dramatic rallies and sell-offs.

- **Emotional gap:** This refers to decision-making based on extreme emotions or emotional strains such as anxiety, anger, fear, or excitement. Often, emotions are a key reason why people do not make rational choices.

- **Anchoring:** Anchoring refers to attaching a spending level to a certain reference. Examples may include spending consistently based on a budget level or rationalising spending based on different satisfaction utilities.

- **Self-attribution:** This is a tendency to make choices based on overconfidence in one's own knowledge or skill. Self-attribution usually stems from an intrinsic knack in a particular area. Within this category, individuals tend to rank their knowledge higher than others, even when it objectively falls short.

Being aware of the precepts of behavioural finance can help investors check their perceptions against facts, a classic example of which is anchoring. This term simply means an investor "anchors" on the price level of a previous portfolio value and constantly compares the previous, often higher, value to the current value without taking into account changes in the market or even outlook.

An investor may also anchor on the price paid for a particular security and refuse to sell it despite poor performance, hoping to at least break even rather than suffer a loss. They do this without carefully assessing the reasons behind that security's loss of value.

Herding is another behaviour to be aware of and to try to avoid in your own investing. Following the crowd is how less sophisticated investors often get into trouble. If "everyone" is buying a particular security, investors often jump in without looking into why (other than the fact its price is rising, because people are buying into it) because they don't want to be left out of a good thing. This is precisely how market and securities "bubbles" form. Herding can also cause an investor to buy into investments that may not be appropriate for their financial goals or risk tolerance.

The reverse can also be true when, for example, a stock market index starts to fall. In this instance, investors want to liquidate their holdings, even in mutual funds, to avoid losses. But a savvy investor can tell that, often, individual securities and markets rise until those who want to buy in do so, and they fall when a few large investors sell.

The reasons behind the movement need to be examined before any investor follows the "herd". This means they need to look for any information available about the company or market beyond the insistence from other investors that "it's going up/

down". Frequently, savvy and large investors sell after a rally to make profits.

High self-rating can also be considered overconfidence. This behaviour often gets investors into trouble as well, because it is founded in the belief that they are smarter or more capable than they actually are, for instance at spotting the next "hot" stock or investment trend. An overconfident investor is often seen trading more frequently than others, believing themselves to have better information than others. Frequent trading often leads to subpar portfolio performance, caused by an increase in commissions, taxes and losses.

These examples highlight why being aware of behavioural finance in an investing context, as well as being aware of both of your own and others' tendencies, can help you save money and look more carefully before leaping into a move or investment.

Other biases revealed by behavioural finance

Breaking down biases further, many individual biases and tendencies have been identified for behavioural finance analysis. Some of these include:

Confirmation bias

Confirmation bias is when investors have a bias toward accepting information that confirms their already-held belief in an investment. If information surfaces, investors accept it readily to confirm that they're correct about their investment decision – even if the information is flawed.

Experiential bias

An experiential bias occurs when investors' memory of recent events makes them biased or leads them to believe that the event is far more likely to occur again. For this reason, it is also known as recency bias or availability bias.

For example, the financial crisis in 2008 and 2009 led many investors to exit the stock market. Many had a dismal view of the markets and likely expected more economic hardship in the coming years. The experience of having gone through such a negative event increased their bias, or likelihood that the event could recur. In reality, the economy recovered, and the market bounced back in the years that followed.

Loss aversion

Loss aversion occurs when investors place a greater weighting on the concern for losses than the pleasure from market gains. In other words, they're far more likely to try to assign a higher priority to avoiding losses than making investment gains. As a result, some investors might want a higher payout to compensate for losses. If the high payout isn't likely, they might try to avoid losses altogether – even if the investment's risk is acceptable from a rational standpoint.

Applying loss aversion to investing leads to the so-called disposition effect which occurs when investors sell their winners and hang onto their losers. Investors' thinking is that they want to realise gains quickly. However, when an investment is losing money, they'll hold onto it because they want to get back to even or their initial price. Investors tend to admit they are correct about an investment quickly (when there's a gain). However, investors are reluctant to admit when they made an investment mistake (when there's a loss). The flaw in disposition bias (or loss aversion) is that the performance of the investment is often anchored to the entry price for the investor, as I explained previously.

Familiarity bias

The familiarity bias is when investors tend to invest in what they know, such as domestic companies or locally owned investments. As a result, investors are not diversified across multiple sectors and types of investments, and thereby not reducing risk. Investors tend to go with investments that they have a history or familiarity with.

The role of emotion and habits

Your financial decisions can also be affected by past experiences, emotions and peer pressure. Emotions drive many of our decisions in life and not only financially. However, there are some financial scenarios where you can see this playing out very clearly.

For example, when the stock market crashed in the UK at the start of the Covid-19 pandemic in 2020, many people sold their positions when the market was at its lowest point. Why did they do that, when there was lots of evidence to show that the market would recover if you just held on? The answer is emotion, and more specifically fear.

Behavioural finance also encompasses your habits surrounding money and your financial life. What small actions do you take regularly that either improve or harm your financial wellbeing? I'll talk in much greater detail about forming good habits around money in Part 2.

What emotions drive financial decisions?

In my experience, fear and greed are the two emotions that are most likely to drive people's financial decision making. Fear is particularly powerful, because it stems from insecurity and a lot of us are very good at spending time in our own heads making ourselves feel insecure. There's no escaping the fact that money is a concern for a lot of people. The challenge is that if you aren't in a sound financial position as a result of the decisions you've made about your finances in the past, it makes it even more difficult to make smart financial decisions in the future.

Greed is the other emotion that often drives financial decision making, which will usually manifest in behaviour like chasing returns. My aim in this instance is to help you work out how much is enough. Again, this stems from insecurity and not knowing how much you need or, possibly, that you already have enough.

Certainty is the antidote to both fear and greed, because when you know what you are trying to achieve it is much easier to make sound financial decisions that move you closer to that goal.

Let's look at investment as an example. If you decide to invest some money without any clear goal in mind around how much you want that investment to earn, it could be very easy to chase ever-higher returns and, in doing so, take on higher levels of risk. Conversely, you might be too risk averse with your investments and therefore be falling short of the returns you need to achieve your goal. However, without knowing what your goal is in either instance, you can't possibly know whether you are on track to hit it or not.

Rather than chasing a nine per cent return and putting your capital at unnecessary risk, you might learn you only need a four per cent return to achieve all you wanted. Or instead of playing it safe with an investment that offers a two per cent return, you might need to take on a little more risk and select an investment offering a four per cent return. Which side of the coin you land on will depend on your own psychology around money and your attitude to investment risk.

As well as a defined goal, you also need to have a good level of understanding about your financial situation and the financial products available to you. This knowledge underpins your decision making and means that you are more likely to make smart decisions more of the time.

Where does peer pressure come into play?

Peer pressure, along with the likes of social proof, can have a bigger impact on financial behaviours than you might imagine. It is very easy to develop a herd mentality, where you follow the crowd rather than analysing the situation and coming to your own conclusion. When you get swept up in this herd mentality, you tend to make purely emotional decisions.

I've seen this at work at live events I've attended. I remember one in particular (run by Anthony Robbins) where they created a "market" that all of us attending were trading on. It all started rather calmly, with people selling items for $1 a piece. Then someone dropped their price to 70 cents and there was a flurry of activity. Then came an announcement that prices across the board would rise by 50 cents, cue another flurry of energetic trading to try and beat the price hike.

It was fascinating to see how people raced around, buying and selling at different prices and making purely emotional decisions because of what else was happening in the room. The point of the exercise was to show how most people make decisions about their money, and when we look at how we behave in modern society you can see clear parallels.

There are people peddling "get rich quick" schemes; there are influencers on social media flaunting their "aspirational" lives; there are people at the pub who are happy to share tips or "advise" you on decisions. It can be very easy to get caught up in these ideas and schemes, and to blindly follow them, without pausing to consider whether this person is a reputable and knowledgeable source of information.

What else affects our financial behaviour?

Confirmation bias is something else to be aware of when it comes to our decision making (not only in relation to finances). As humans, we tend to only look for and accept information we agree with, and ignore everything else. This means the information we see confirms our decisions, rather than challenges them. This can, naturally, be dangerous if what you believe is not beneficial for your financial situation, because you are unlikely to seek out information to help you challenge and reframe that belief.

Often these are beliefs that we have carried with us for much of our lives, in many cases that have been passed on from generation to generation, and because they are so deep-rooted they can be difficult to shift.

One that I commonly encounter is the belief that investing in property is the only way to make money. In my experience, many people like property as an asset because they can see and feel it and they understand it. Don't get me wrong, property investing is not necessarily a bad option, but it isn't the only option. Diversifying your investments is important not only to ensure you don't have all your eggs in one basket, but also due to tax consequences.

However, I have spoken to property investors in the past about diversifying their portfolio away from property and their immediate reaction is to distrust the alternatives, because they don't understand them and believe that they carry greater risk. In a lot of cases, these people also feel like they have control over their property investments, whereas if they were to invest in, for example, stocks, they would have to give control of their investments to someone else. Even if that person is a specialist in what they do, this idea of relinquishing control doesn't sit well with them. This then drives the behaviour of continuing to invest in property rather than diversifying.

This is just one example to illustrate how our beliefs and emotions can affect our behaviour. How this plays out in your life will be different to how it plays out in someone else's. Start thinking about some of the decisions you make and why you are making them. Can you see any gaps in your knowledge? Are you attached to a particular type of investment for emotional, rather than rational, reasons?

Taking control of your financial behaviour

If, as you've been reading this chapter, you can see that you have been influenced by others, or you are starting to recognise you may hold some beliefs that have been holding you back, this is a good opportunity to pause and check in with yourself. Are there any areas where you would benefit from educating yourself? How is it best to do that? Could working with professionals in a specific area be the best option for you?

Building a team of people around you who are experienced in areas where you lack knowledge, is one of the best behavioural habits you can develop in relation to your finances. The key is to be open to alternative ideas and knowledge that can help you make decisions based on facts, rather than beliefs or trends.

Getting to know yourself

Understanding yourself is essential to this process, however, because it is only in understanding what your beliefs and biases are that you can determine whether they are helpful or harmful, and look at how to change the ones that are holding you back.

Whenever I see a new client, I take them through a whole questionnaire that is designed to explore their history of financial decision making and help them get to know themselves. During this process, I simulate financial decisions by asking what they would do in certain scenarios, as well as running through a personality questionnaire. The aim is that by the end of this process, you have a better understanding of your behaviour in relation to your finances and how you make financial decisions.

Creating a plan for your finances is particularly important because this gives you the certainty and sense of security you need to avoid making emotional decisions or getting sucked into that herd mentality I talked about earlier. Even when the world is going mad, you can come back to your plan and know that by sticking to it you are making the best financial decisions for your long-term gain.

Having this level of clarity also enables you to spot opportunities that you might otherwise miss. When your mind is free of emotional "clutter" and you don't feel stressed about your finances, you are much more likely to see opportunities and to be able to take them.

Your values are also important here, because you want to make sure your financial decisions align with those values and allow you to remain true to yourself. This will allow you to make decisions that are based on what's truly important to you, rather than what's going on in the world around you.

Being aware of your values also ensures you can avoid conflict further down the line when you realise that some of your behaviour isn't aligned with your deepest values and goals. For example, if one of your goals is to make the world a better, more environmentally conscious place for your family, but the majority of your investments are in oil companies, your financial decisions in that respect aren't aligned to your goal of wanting to make the world a better, more sustainable place. In this instance, it's likely that you would need to change your investments to ensure they aligned with that goal and your deeper values.

The benefits of working with experts

We all know that having an external perspective can help in many areas of our lives and it's really no different with your finances. In fact, research shows there are significant benefits to working with a financial planner, beyond the financial returns of having their expertise at your disposal. I'll talk specifically about the non-financial benefits of working with a financial planner in Part 3. Essentially though, these benefits stem from having someone to guide you and help you make smart decisions. It is really invaluable to have someone who will encourage you to hold your nerve when markets are rocky, as well as help you stay on track with your financial plan and take opportunities when they arise.

Working with a financial planner also helps you create positive behaviours around your finances. For example, just sitting down and regularly reviewing your position is an incredibly positive behaviour and one that will mean you are much more likely to stay on track than if you don't check in with your progress regularly.

This value extends beyond your finances to your general approach to life and decision making, because having that expert to act as a sounding board means you're far less likely to get sucked in by fake or sensationalist news or follow the crowd. Instead, you're cultivating a well-rounded and well-educated view of the world and using this as the basis for your decision making, alongside your personal values and goals.

Finding the balance between your current self and your future self

Whenever you're making financial decisions, it's important to ensure there is a balance between your current self and your future self. You don't want to focus so much on the here and now that you're storing up problems for your future self, but equally you don't want to be so fixated on the future that you forget to enjoy your life now.

Keep one eye on today, because that's all we have; but keep one eye on the future too, because that will become your today. It's important to remember you can't give up everything from today just for tomorrow, because that's no fun and you have to have some fun along the way! But you also don't want to be looking back in 20 years' time, regretting a string of poor decisions made by your past self. As with most things in life, this is about striking the right balance. This, again, is where working with a financial planner can be very valuable.

I use planning and cash flow modelling tools that take your values, goals and finances, model them into the future and check that you're on track with what you want to achieve. Once you have done this exercise, it only requires an annual or biannual check-in with your financial planner to make sure you're still on track and to tweak anything that isn't quite aligned to your goals.

Continually reviewing your financial plan is important; there is no point in writing one only to stick it in a drawer and never look at it again. Similarly, there's no point in having a vision for what an abundant life looks like to you, only to hide it away and never read it. Regularly reviewing your situation is one of the most positive behavioural habits you can develop.

Gratitude is also important, because there can certainly be a tendency in the Western World to take what we have for granted when, in monetary terms, we are already incredibly wealthy. Building gratitude into our lives and recognising all that we do have is another powerful tool you can use.

The positive behaviour loop

When you start to build these positive behaviours, they feed into one another and the whole thing snowballs. As you become more aware of your financial position, you're creating certainty about where you are. This gives you security and as you build your wealth and achieve your goals, that certainty grows. This helps encourage you to keep doing all those positive behaviours, because they create the certainty that was lacking for you in the past.

This allows you to learn from your past decisions, and having a plan gives you a sense of direction and purpose. Knowing what direction you're travelling in allows you to make more informed decisions about the best route to follow. It also encourages you to examine your decisions and be conscious of when you might need more information, education or an external perspective from an expert to help you on your way. Underpinning all of this is the certainty you get from having a plan to follow. Knowing where this is leading allows you to observe and examine external events and opportunities without bringing emotion into the equation, and that in turn means you are likely to make much sounder financial decisions.

A piece of the puzzle

I talked in the introduction about the concept of having a jigsaw puzzle of your life, where you are missing pieces and also clarity over what the picture will look like once it's completed. Everything I've discussed so far in this book are essential pieces of your puzzle. Understanding your beliefs around money, how and why you make certain financial decisions, and what you value in life and therefore what goals are most important to you is incredibly empowering.

Behavioural finance explores why you make the decisions you make and seeks to help you see what underpins your behaviour. This allows you to make meaningful changes to your relationship with money, because you can see what beliefs or past experiences cause you to make certain decisions around your finances and, if they are holding you back, you have the power to change them.

Part 1: Your Reality of the Past

Part 2

THE PRESENT

In the first part of the book, I encouraged you to examine your past to start uncovering what your beliefs about money and wealth are and where they come from. With this new-found understanding of why you behave in certain ways when it comes to your finances, as well as what potentially false beliefs you have around not only money, but also wealth, you are on the route to building up a comprehensive picture of what real wealth looks like to you and how you can achieve it.

As you move into Part 2, I'm going to invite you to take a deep dive on your current position and make sure that you are very clear about where you are, right now. You can't plan the best route to a destination if you don't know where you're starting from, so in the coming chapters I'd like you to be honest about your current position and start to think about what habits and behaviours you could change from this moment forward.

This isn't only about your finances, but also about your thinking. In fact, getting your mindset right is the key to unlocking your potential and is a vital piece of your wealth puzzle. When you start to think about a situation in the right way, solutions and opportunities will present themselves, even if all you saw before were problems and opportunities.

I'll also help you work out what you already know about your financial situation and where there might be some gaps, as well as providing some practical suggestions of positive financial habits that you can start to introduce to your life if they will support you on your journey.

At the end of this part, I'll share the wealth bucket exercise that I use with my clients to help them build up a detailed and honest picture of their finances. This also allows you to see where money may be leaking from your bucket and therefore what steps you can take to plug those leaks. You might be surprised by how much you can save simply by completing this one exercise. But let's not get ahead of ourselves, first you have to make sure your mindset and thinking is in the right place, because this is what will give you a strong foundation on which to build real wealth and the future you truly desire.

Chapter 3
KNOWN UNKNOWNS

Many of us have gaps in our financial knowledge through no fault of our own and the reason is that we are not deliberately taught about finances or what true wealth means during our lives. In many cases, we collect financial knowledge from those around us and that means what we learn will be limited by the people we know, unless we go out of our way to seek out experts who can help educate us on areas we don't fully understand.

An analogy I like to use is that of a jigsaw puzzle, as I explained in the introduction. When it comes to finances, we go through our lives picking up pieces of information here and there. You might learn about different financial products, like mortgages or ISAs, and start using them. You'll likely have a pension set up through your workplace and you'll be paying into it. If you run your own business, you might have limited knowledge of your accounts and tax position.

However, all you have are pieces of the puzzle, you don't have a completed jigsaw and you don't have oversight of the whole picture.

I often ask people, "When you're given a jigsaw puzzle, where do you start?" Most people's response is, "With the corner pieces." However, none of us start in the corners; we start by looking at the picture itself. It's only when you can see what the completed picture should look like that you can start to see how all of those pieces you've been collecting fit together.

Picking up the pieces

As we move through our lives, we continually pick up pieces of our jigsaw puzzle that are related to our finances. I often speak to clients who have a lot of the financial pieces of their puzzle in place. They have investments and savings; they have a pension; they have a mortgage. In other cases, I speak to people who struggle to budget and who constantly find there's more and more month at the end of the money. What they all lack, regardless of what state their finances are currently in, is a strategy. This means they don't fully understand how the decisions they make today will affect their future.

They have some of the pieces, they may even have started putting their jigsaw together, but they are lacking a crucial overview of the whole picture and this is what's holding them back. They don't know how much is "enough" and they don't know how much money they will need in the future. Pensions are a classic example of this. We are all told we should put money into a pension, and many of us do, but very few stop to work out how much we need to pay into a pension to ensure we have "enough" when the time comes to retire.

It's very easy to bury your head in the sand when it comes to planning for your financial future. For many it is always something that can be dealt with another time because retirement is still years away. I know one couple who have a degree of certainty with their pensions, because one is a firefighter and the other works as a medical professional in the NHS. However, despite the fact that they have pensions in place, they have no idea how much they'll need in retirement. They have been putting off working this out for years, but they are inching closer to retirement and answering that question is becoming more pressing.

Piecing together the picture

This lack of clarity is one of the biggest issues that stems from picking up all these pieces of financial information without thinking about how they fit into the jigsaw puzzle that is your life, both now and in the future. There is so much noise out there that it's easy to see why so many people go through life without even thinking about answering this question, let alone knowing where to find the answers from.

This is why it's so beneficial to work with someone like a financial planner who can take a step back and help you see your bigger picture. They can ask you questions like, "What's important to you? What does a good lifestyle look like to you going forward? What do you want for your future?" Once they have the answers to those questions, they can crunch the numbers and tell you how much you need financially to achieve the lifestyle you want. A financial planner can also advise you about how to organise your affairs in the most efficient way.

However, the most important thing a financial planner will do is help you gain clarity about what your big picture looks like and help you see that real wealth is about far more than your finances. Often people will come to me because they have a financial problem that needs to be solved or there has been an event in their lives, like receiving an inheritance or selling their business, which means they want some guidance around their money. What I do is take a comprehensive approach to each situation and make sure that both the client and I understand what their bigger picture looks like, because it's only once we can see the picture we're trying to create that we can work out how all the pieces of the puzzle slot together.

This involves a much bigger discussion about what real wealth, their ideal life in the future and a successful life looks like to them. Only once we both know that can we organise their money, because their finances need to be arranged to create this picture.

You don't know what you don't know

The challenge is that you don't know what you don't know, which means it's my job to help educate you (and all my clients) about where you might have gaps in your knowledge and then to help you fill those gaps in so that you can clearly piece together your bigger picture. To reach this point, you have to be open to having a conversation that zooms you out of the details and the individual pieces of your puzzle that focus on your finances, and shows you what that picture looks like.

When you are able to do this, not only do you get clarity about what your future can, and does, look like, but you will also be open-minded to suggestions and recommendations of how you can achieve that picture if you're not already on course for it.

This can be a challenge at times, because the financial services industry has spent years teaching us to focus on money and equating the amount of money in our bank accounts with wealth. However, as you know, the reality is that money is simply a facilitator, allowing you to achieve the life you want.

Many of the clients I speak to know they have gaps in their knowledge, but they don't know where to start when it comes to putting the pieces of their puzzle together. This is why being able to see your big picture is so important. If I gave you a 500-piece jigsaw puzzle but no picture of what it should look like, you would be uncertain about where it was best to start. However, if you had a picture in front of you it would be a lot easier and quicker to not only get started, but also to put those pieces together.

As I've said, you have been collecting the pieces of your jigsaw puzzle your whole life, but what you're missing is that picture. This is what I'd like to help you find.

It's a similar story for many people who own a business. They don't always have clarity about what they want their business to look like. One of the most important questions to ask yourself if you're a business owner is: have you got the business that you set out to create? What often happens is that entrepreneurs create a business plan for the bank. Once again, the action they take is related solely to money, in this case raising finance for their business. What they don't have is a clear plan for what they want their business to look like and how they fit into that business.

You might have all your cash flow and profit and loss projections in order for the bank, but have you stopped to ask yourself what you want your business to look like in three, five or ten years? Do you know where your business fits into your wheel of wealth?

Stepping off the treadmill

Often I meet people who are on what I describe as the business treadmill. They are working day in, day out without stopping to think about who they're doing it for and why. A business should be a vehicle you can use to get what you want out of life, but all too often it becomes a grindstone and, in some cases, an entrepreneur's quality of life will be worse than if they just had a regular job.

Some people love running their own business: it's their passion and it's what drives them. Work can be the same for people who are employed. However, there are plenty of people in this world for whom work is a chore, a means to pay the bills and have the odd holiday, nothing more. If your business feels like this, then you have likely lost your way somewhere along your journey. Often, when you start to unpick this, you can see that it's a case of having conflicting values.

Many businesspeople will tell me that they started their business because they wanted to be independent, have freedom and achieve X, Y and Z. When I take them out of the day to day, what we often discover is that they work long hours, don't take as many holidays as they intend to and don't have the free time they'd like. In some cases, these people are working long past the point at which they need to, from a financial perspective.

This is why it's so important to be clear about how much is enough, and this applies whether you run your own business or are employed by someone else. Having clarity about how much is enough to live the life you want, and knowing either that you have reached it or when you will reach it, is incredibly empowering.

Some people discover through this process that they have more than enough and they act on it and make changes to their lives. Others discover they have more than enough but want to keep going and this in itself tells you what's important to you. However, this generally opens up a conversation about a sense of uncertainty over what they'll do with their time if they exit their business or stop working – but this is very different to continuing to work because you need to financially. At this point it becomes a choice and that is very freeing.

This process is about taking you from a place of uncertainty to a place of certainty. The peace of mind you gain from knowing that financially you're in a good position, is massive. Even if you aren't where you want to be just yet, you will see that you have choices and you will know exactly what you need to do to achieve the picture you have in mind for your life. Either way, it's the clarity that empowers you and encourages you to take positive action.

When you go through this process, you will likely have a series of lightbulb moments, on one level relating to your values and how you can align your goals and your money with them; and on another level in relation to your financial situation. In my experience, there are three scenarios I see clients in: they're not OK but they've now realised they need to do something about it; they're just about OK but could do a bit more; or they already have more than they'll ever need and can get on with living the life they want.

In some cases, the people who fall into that last category are still chasing money and this usually stems from feelings of insecurity around their finances. They may have a scarcity mentality in relation to money that they're not consciously aware of. Often a scarcity mentality relating to money will come from having an upbringing where there was always insecurity around finances.

Paul's story: childhood money lessons

When I was young, my dad left my mother, my two siblings and me, and we had to fend for ourselves for a while. During this period, money was really scarce. We went from being in quite a comfortable situation to being in a very uncomfortable one. That meant I understood the value of money, and the scarcity of it, for a period of my life.

I also learnt some very important money lessons from my mother, one of which was the importance of saving. She always saved, even when there wasn't much left to save and she encouraged me and my siblings to do the same. I feel very fortunate that I learnt this lesson at a young age and that I acted on it. You see so many people nowadays who are living beyond their means.

There's a "buy now, pay later!" mentality that encourages people to get into debt, rather than saving money to make a purchase.

This ties back into the concept of behavioural finance, demonstrating how we learn from those around us and how this knowledge translates into our behaviour. Once you become aware of the habits you have with your money, you can explore how to create new habits that will be more beneficial. This is a topic I'll come back to in Chapter 5.

As a brief example of the kind of habit you can easily automate, however, I have a question for you. Imagine that in the last ten years, you had only lived on 90 per cent of your net income and saved the remainder. Would you have starved, gone bankrupt and really struggled? Or would you have been OK, still had your holidays and not really missed that money? Assuming it's the latter, just think about how much you would now have saved, without having changed the quality of your life materially in the last decade. Saving in this way is simple, because all you do is put ten per cent of your pay cheque into savings as soon as it arrives in your bank. It's the age-old lesson of "pay yourself first". When you do this, you find yourself in a much better place.

How to create behavioural change

One of the best ways to change your behaviour is to set goals and create a comprehensive plan for every aspect of your life. I know this from my own experience, as well as from what I see working for my clients. In the next chapter I'll share a story about how my business almost went under after a failed acquisition of part of it. Briefly, the difference came when I changed my thinking, because this was what allowed me to focus on the solutions rather than the problems I was facing. The solution was based on thinking about what my business had to look like for it to be successful.

I created a vision for what my business would look like and a vision for what my personal life would look like, using a template from a book called *The E Myth*[7] by Michael E. Gerber. I wrote my first vision in 2007 and I have updated it every year since. My business vision is a rolling three-year document and this links into my life vision. Using both of these documents as the model, I create my own financial plan, looking at the resources I have now and the resources I might have in the future to make sure I stay on track.

When I think back to my business challenges, I know those problems weren't solved overnight, but having a compelling vision for the future allowed me to see that I could get both what I wanted and the business I wanted by helping others do the same. I followed the same process for myself as I do for my clients, piecing together my own jigsaw once I'd seen the bigger picture.

7   Michael E. Gerber, (2001), The E Myth Revisited: Why Most Small Businesses Don't Work and What to Do About It, HarperBus, updated subsequent edition

Spotting the signs that you need support

For many people, there won't necessarily be a crisis in their lives that prompts them to reevaluate the track they are on, like I had to. However, there will still be signs that your life could be better and that you could feel more fulfilled both personally and professionally.

Although everyone's circumstances will be different, some of the most common scenarios I encounter with my clients who are business owners are that they aren't as tax efficient as they could be. Their accountant may have structured their finances to allow them to extract money from the business, but it's unlikely that they have talked to the business owner about making the most of their pension contributions, for example. This may mean there is cash sitting in the business that I describe as "lazy cash" because it's not making any money for them.

In some cases, the business owner is fearful of extracting more money from their business than they currently do because they worry they will be taxed on it. While this might be true, in some cases they can claim some of that tax back and still invest the money to ensure it's working for them in the longer term. If this sounds familiar to you, I would advise you to engage a financial planner who can help you find the missing pieces of your jigsaw and connect them to build that whole picture. A financial planner will work with your accountant to structure a joined-up plan and they'll work with you to ensure you're making smart decisions for both your business and your personal life.

Terry: the road to financial freedom

Terry is on the verge of selling his business and he's ready to retire. At the age of 56 he's financially free, and he can't wait for the next chapter of his life to begin.

Throughout his life, Terry focused on getting rid of his debt. He also preferred to keep cash in the bank, rather than invest it, which meant that he ultimately lost out because the interest paid on his capital didn't keep pace with inflation. However, despite all the advice explaining this to him, he was always adamant that he wanted the cash in the bank because it gave him a sense of security.

Over many years, with careful education about the different kinds of investments he could use and how they work, he gradually started to shift some of his cash into pensions, ISAs and other investments. This has helped him achieve his goals.

However, the main factor that has allowed Terry to sell his business and achieve financial freedom at 56 is that he's had a plan in place for more than ten years. This plan is based around helping him and his wife achieve the life they want. Once his business sale goes through, he plans to take a few months off and then return to work part time.

Being wary of investment, like Terry was, is a common sign that you would benefit from the support of a financial planner too. Many people don't understand where their money will be invested and they worry about losing everything and going bust. When you see headlines like the ones appearing in the news at the start of the Covid-19 pandemic, when billions were wiped off the value of the stock market in a matter of days, it's understandable why people become fearful of investing.

Financial markets are complex and there is far more nuance to investment than what's plastered all over the news. It's my role as a financial planner to not only help you understand that, but also to simplify this complex world and educate you so that you can make informed decisions and move away from unfounded insecurities.

Although I've talked about business owners being wary of being taxed too much, this is something that many people worry about. However, with the support of a financial planner you can take some simple steps to reduce your taxation legally, now and in the future.

Your evolving plan

Creating a plan for your future, both financially and in every area of your life, is not an exercise you do once and put to one side. As I've explained, you need to update your plan regularly as your life and goals change. I'm a big advocate of living for today and enjoying the journey, but whilst keeping one eye on the future. That's what a plan helps you to do.

Often, there is a sense of conflict between the you of today and the 60-year-old you who's waiting in the future. A good exercise is to imagine how a conversation between yourself now and your 60-year-old self would go. Would your 60-year-old self be thanking you for some of the decisions you're making now, or would they be asking why you didn't make any provision for that future?

You have to evaluate the decisions you're making now based on what you've learnt in the past and decide whether what you learnt is helping or hindering you. Try to understand why you are where you are today, and think about how the decisions you make now will affect your future. Visualise your future and your 60-year-old self and think about the position they will be in as a result of the decisions you're making in the present.

Your plan and your understanding of where you're heading will change as things happen in your life. There is one couple I've worked with for many years and I helped their daughter map out her picture. She was very successful in her career, with no sign of an impending wedding or talk of children on the horizon. All of a sudden, she met the love of her life, got married, had a child and now we're putting together their picture of life as a family. You have to update your picture as your life changes and that will enable you to keep working towards the future you want to live.

Rebecca and David: a sudden change

David and Rebecca had been together almost eight years, and living together for six. They had met later in life and both had children from previous relationships. Rebecca is a long-time family friend of mine. David worked in a senior management role for a well-known electronics company and their lifestyle had always given the impression of being comfortable – regular holidays, eating out several times a week, changing cars regularly, treating friends and family generously and, of course, always owning the latest must-have gadget.

They had talked about getting married for several years and had saved a deposit as they were considering buying a house together – in short, they were building what looked like a comfortable future together. I had offered several times to help them build a plan to better understand their current position and what they really wanted to achieve, but they had always declined, insisting they would sort all of that out once they found the "right" house to buy. However, before that could happen, tragedy struck.

David passed away unexpectedly and I found myself trying to sort out his estate with Rebecca.

She had made a list of all the bills and services held in David's name, but it took almost a whole day just to organise all the information about his bank accounts, savings, investments and pensions. They had one joint account together, from which they paid the bills, but the bulk of the money that was paid in came from David's sole account, into which his salary was paid. Rebecca worked part-time in an administration role in the NHS, so David was the main provider for their household.

I wanted to support my friend in this time of great uncertainty and sadness, so together we started building a list of what needed to be done. The home they lived in was rented in David's name, so the first task was to transfer the tenancy to her, although it was far from certain whether she could afford the rent alone.

As well as never having married, there was an additional complication – David had not made a will. This meant that his two children (aged 19 and 21 at the time) were made executors under the laws of intestacy. However, understandably they didn't feel equipped to handle this, so they gave authority to David's brother to act in this capacity.

Although Rebecca knew David's brother well, this didn't stop her feeling left out of the whole process. The home they had together, the plans they had made (or at least considered) and the future imagined were gone – nothing was in her control.

While David had spoken to his employers about naming Rebecca on his company pension, they couldn't find any instruction to do so. In addition to his pension, death in service benefits and also his outstanding earnings were to be paid, but it was uncertain who should receive these.

All David's savings, investments and the monies they had earmarked as a house deposit were in his sole name. He had made no separate life or critical illness provisions and was paying only the basic pension contribution through his employer. Whether he made this decision because he had a very good salary and always believed they would be OK, I cannot say.

As you can well imagine, the following few months were very stressful. Although my friend still lives in the home they had together, along with her two children, she now works full time and all thoughts of buying her own home are no longer a consideration. She is still in regular contact with David's family, and they all got together a year after his passing to spread his ashes and celebrate his life.

Rebecca did receive a modest sum from David's pension in the end, but as they weren't married there was no spouse's pension under the terms of the plan. It was a one-off payment that, while enough to allow her to be comfortable for a few years, amounted to little more.

All his pensions, savings and investments were otherwise split between his two children, and David's ex-wife (their mother) is overseeing what they spend their inheritance on for the most part – which, we are sure, is not what David would have wanted.

I have never commented to my friend or her family about how much of what occurred following David's death could have been avoided, and I do not wish to be critical now. However, I truly believe this is a situation that many people are in danger of experiencing and I would like this to act as a cautionary tale of the transience of wealth being dependent upon effective planning. The true cost of not taking some time to plan can be far more than most people imagine.

I sincerely hope that, on reading this, you do not believe I sat back and let this happen to a long-time family friend, with no regard for the uncertainty of their position. In fact, over the years I lost count of how many times I offered to help or suggested they look at making their situation more certain. All to no avail. With hindsight, if I had been more insistent would things have been different?

This, I believe, hits the heart of the matter: YOU have to choose to take action, and do so long before the worst might possibly happen.

A piece of the puzzle

It's important to acknowledge that you don't know what you don't know and to therefore seek out the support of professionals who can help you fill in the gaps in your knowledge. Many of us lack any formal financial education, which is why support in this area of your life can be particularly beneficial.

When you're putting together the pieces of your personal jigsaw puzzle, it's essential to know what the picture looks like. This should be a picture of your future and this is why the support of a financial planner can be so valuable. You see, a financial planner has their own version of a crystal ball on their desk and they look to the future, rather than just examining the past. This future focus is crucial for building a plan and setting goals to achieve the life you want.

It's equally important to make sure you're regularly reviewing your plan to ensure it still matches up with the vision you have for your future, however, because our lives change and sometimes we can change course when we least expect it. Nevertheless, one of the most important things a financial planner can do for you, is help you challenge and change your thinking when it's not serving you or your business, which is what I'll explore in more detail in the next chapter.

Chapter 4
STATE OF MIND AND MINDSET

There are two aspects of state of mind that I'm going to explore in this chapter: the mindset of your adviser and your mindset. However, before I look at both of those in a bit more detail, I'd like to introduce you to the Three Principles. This is a concept I learnt from John Dashfield, author of *The Client-centred Financial Adviser*[8], and these principles relate to how we experience life in general, not just our finances.

These Three Principles are:

1. Mind

2. Consciousness

3. Thinking

Mind is sometimes referred to as intelligence, the universe and even God, depending on who you speak to. Essentially "mind" is the energy all around us that we don't have to think about. For

---

8   John Dashfield, (2015), The Client-centred Financial Adviser: The ultimate guide to building high-trust, high-profit relationships and a thriving practice, SRA Books

example, if I cut my finger I don't have to think about how it's going to heal, it's just going to heal. Trees grow throughout their lives; they get new shoots of growth in the spring, they continue to grow throughout the summer and in the autumn they shed their leaves in time for winter. This is the intelligence of life.

Often we measure intelligence in terms of IQ and we forget that we all have this innate wellbeing and intelligence within us, we just don't necessarily know (or need to know) how it works.

Consciousness is our ability to be aware of what's going on around us, what we're experiencing and what we're thinking. The more conscious we can be, the more clarity we have about what's going on around us.

Thinking refers to the thousands of thoughts we have every day. The quality of our thoughts significantly impacts the quality of our lives. We all have good and bad thoughts and it's our thoughts that create our feelings. You can't have a feeling without a thought and as soon as you understand this, you begin to realise the power you have to control your experience of the world. The old adage, "I think, therefore I am" certainly holds true in this instance.

Albert Einstein is believed to have said, "We cannot solve our problems with the same thinking we used when we created them," and this is true of all of life's problems. The truth is that our problems around money are really only perceived problems, and it's our thinking that makes us see them as problems rather than being able to see the solutions.

As an example, when I ask clients what money means to them, they will often answer something like, "Security". However, whether money means security or insecurity to someone is down to their thinking around it, rather than the money itself. As the Three Principles show us, everything we perceive externally in our environment actually comes from within ourselves.

The mindset of the adviser (me)

When you go to see a financial adviser, their mindset is paramount to the experience you will have. In this situation, I act as a facilitator to help you navigate your way through life from a financial perspective. I'm here to help you uncover what money means to you and how you use money to facilitate what you want out of life. If I'm going to help you answer these questions, it's vital that I have clarity of mind and am fully present. Having a clear mind is what allows me to be truly client centred, which is at the heart of the philosophy at my business.

The reason is simple: my state of mind affects my client's state of mind. When I am present, it makes them more present and when you're more present, you have greater clarity and are able to come up with new ideas and solutions. When my mindset is in the right place, I am able to facilitate a high-quality conversation with my clients.

Whether a conversation I have with a client is powerful or not is dictated by how the client feels during our conversation – but what affects how the client feels? The answer is the practitioner (in this case me) and the "feeling state" I'm in. Why is this so? Because it will affect the tone of the conversation. This means what I say is less important than where it comes from.

Prominent psychologist Dr. George Pransky, author of *The Relationship Handbook*[9], said, "Listen for the spirit behind the communication. When you are touched by feelings, you have gotten what that person has tried to say. You will feel enriched and the other person will feel heard." There is scientific evidence to support the fact that the state of mind the practitioner is in will affect both the nature of the conversation and the relationship they have with a given client.

Our brains contain what are known as "mirror neurons", which are so named because they "mirror" the neurology of the person

---

9   Dr. George Pransky, (2017), The Relationship Handbook: A Simple Guide to Satisfying Relationships, Pransky & Associates, Anniversary edition

we are communicating with. We are blessed with many of these "mirror neurons"; in fact, they make up one third of our neurons.

It is believed that these neurons are what allow us to experience empathy. It is our ability to feel other people's emotions and the intentions behind their words that make it incredibly difficult for any of us to convincingly fake deep emotions.

Being fully present is also important in terms of helping us connect with people. It makes the process of connection almost effortless and we are much less likely to be attached to the outcome of an interaction. This also means our behaviour is much less likely to be controlling, because this tendency stems from fear, rather than a place of feeling secure. This is a healthy state of mind.

To help encourage myself and the other advisers at my firm to be fully present and client centred in all meetings, we have thrown away agendas, because they encourage us to focus on information that isn't necessarily relevant or useful rather than focusing all our attention on each client. When you have a clear mind and you're more present, the answers you need will come to you. This ensures I am able to help each of my clients to the best of my ability.

The mindset of the client (you)

Your mindset as a client is equally important in these interactions, because as I have just explained, when your mind is clear and you're present, answers will come to you. Not only this, however, but you will see endless opportunities. If you feel insecure about money, one of the best ways to move towards a feeling of security is to understand that there are opportunities all around. Often the reason you don't see these opportunities is that your head is elsewhere (you don't have a clear mind).

We all know that when we go to see a coach, they aren't going to give us the answers; they are going to facilitate a conversation that allows us to come up with the answers ourselves. It's no different when a client comes to see me about their financial situation. All the answers they need are already within their reach, it's simply my role to help them see these for themselves.

As an adviser, my role is to help you examine your perceptions of your world and see how these perceptions are shaping your present. You get what you pay attention to, so if you are focusing on not having enough money in retirement and needing to earn more, you will always be trapped on that hamster wheel of thinking you need to work longer and harder to achieve a perceived level of financial wealth before you can retire.

It can be very easy to spend your life in a constant state of busyness, filling your mind with un-useful information from the internet, TV, news outlets. There is more information available in the world than ever before, in fact there is too much information available, which contributes to most people's state of mind being the poorest it has ever been.

Very often, this means a client will attend a meeting with their mind full of this information. As an adviser, I have to help them find clarity and I can only do that if I have a clear mind myself. The beauty is that when they find that clarity, they can make great decisions and this improves their state of mind. Ultimately this leads to them understanding that their reality is their thinking around money and finances and therefore that they have the ability to improve their situation.

Paul's story: clearing the fog of confusion

I know the value that finding clarity in a challenging situation can bring because I have been there myself. There's one story in particular that I'd like to share with you now – I mentioned it briefly in the last chapter. Let's step back to 2006...

I've just sold half my business to a multi-service accountancy firm. It feels like a very exciting time. I have expanded the business significantly and taken on a number of new staff. Everything appears to be going really well until 18 months after the sale. The accountancy firm is in serious financial trouble; the business is being acquired and I'm suddenly left in a position where I have to untangle the half of the business I sold and bring it back under my roof. Not only that, but we are in the midst of the 2007 global financial crisis, one of the biggest financial meltdowns in decades.

Despite all of this, I kept a positive mindset and told myself that it didn't matter. We would plough on, I'd keep the new staff I'd hired and the business would be fine, even though we were in significant debt. I wasn't only building up business debt, but also personal debt because I was having to put money into the business to pay the wages. Despite my best efforts to remain positive, my thinking was entirely focused on the fact that we were sliding deeper and deeper into debt.

I spent all my time looking at cash flow sheets and my head was full of the perceived problems we had as a business. I was constantly looking at the numbers and the more I looked at them, the worse they got. I was in a constant state of stress. At the time, my perception was that the situation was creating this feeling, but looking back I can see that it was my thinking around what was happening that was creating my stress. Everything in my life was affected by my thinking and my stress.

This continued for quite some time, until one day I had a moment of clarity. I realised that instead of focusing on the problems, I needed to focus on the solutions and look at the opportunities we had as a business. At that moment, it was as though the fog lifted. Suddenly I could see a path forward.

I created a plan that focused on how I could get the business (and therefore myself) out of debt. I focused on what I could control and accepted what I couldn't control, like the recession and economic situation. As soon as I made this shift in my thinking, things started to happen that were positive for the business. I had avoided making any redundancies – because I wanted to look after my staff – but then one of my team decided to move to Canada and another one chose to leave the business. My wage bill reduced and my ducks started to line up.

All that changed was my thinking about the situation, which allowed me to start seeing solutions where previously all I'd seen were debts stacking up. Remember that quote I shared earlier? You can't solve a problem with the same thinking that created it. It took around two years to bring the business back to a strong position, but the change in my thinking took just seconds.

As it turned out, there were solutions all around me, my thinking had just been so clouded before that I couldn't see them.

While that is my story about how a shift in my thinking made a big difference to the outcomes I was seeing in my life, there are many more stories in the world of people who have had a similar moment of clarity and been able to change their thinking and therefore their situation as a result.

I was able to come to that realisation myself, but for many people it requires the support of someone external to see that fog of confusion lift. This is why I have spent time in this chapter talking about the mindset of the adviser, as well as of you as a client, because both are fundamental for facilitating this kind of shift in thinking.

Approaching problems from the right mindset

In 2020 a child psychologist came to me for help. His thinking was that he couldn't afford to retire. In fact, he didn't want to retire fully, he just wanted to move away from the management role he had found himself in and go back to being a practitioner where he could help more children. He also had a life-limiting illness and children of his own with whom he wanted to spend more time.

When he came to see me, he had no solutions for his problems. He didn't have a pot of money to invest. All he had were problems and although he knew he wanted a change, he couldn't see how to achieve that.

Because my mindset was in the right place for our meeting, I was able to facilitate a very high-quality conversation with him. He visibly started to relax as we spoke and as he got into the flow of the meeting we started to talk around some of his problems and the potential solutions to help him create a better life and achieve what he wanted. By the time he arrived for his second meeting with me, we were able to create a plan to support the life he wanted to live.

We spent time reorganising his affairs and in doing so I was able to show him that, financially, he was okay. We put together a number of cash flow forecasts that looked at scenarios like paying off his mortgage and taking some of his retirement benefits now. However, the real power in what I was able to do with him didn't come from the cash flow forecasts, it came from me having understood his situation and his thinking around his situation, and helping him see that everything he wanted was possible without having to work harder or longer. The power came from helping him to change his thinking.

Roland's story

Two relatively short meetings with Paul changed my life. I learned that I could retire and create a whole new lifestyle for myself and my loved ones. I had expected an administratively and financially driven meeting, focusing solely on stats, data, and figures. In fact. Paul took time to learn about my hopes, ambitions, priorities, and limitations. The discussions with Paul inspired me to make incredible changes to my lifestyle. I learned that my long-term finances were sustainable. This provided me with the confidence to retire and take my 10-year-old daughter, Alice, around the world as a start to my new life. I am indebted to Paul for taking the time to listen to my dreams and for matching them to my long-term finances.

Digging deeper into your thinking

Every conversation I have with each of my clients will be different. I don't have a set list of questions that I ask, because when I have a clear state of mind the right questions to ask each person will just come to me and they'll help facilitate the conversation, whatever direction it needs to go in. However, many of my questions focus on trying to get each individual to think more deeply about why they want to take a particular course of action (or not). One conversation starter might be, "When you think about money, what's important to you?" Once someone has given me their answer, I may follow that up with, "Understanding that, can you tell me a bit more about why that's so important to you?" It's this focus on the why that brings people closer to clarity.

Let's look at an example to see how this might play out and how understanding your why might affect your decision.

Jenny has come to see me because she's inherited some money. Like a lot of people, her goal is to be debt free and she's considering using that lump sum to pay off her mortgage. "I know I should probably invest the money I've inherited because I'll get a better return on it," she tells me, "but I'd just like to be mortgage free." Investing the money is the logical approach, particularly at the time of writing in 2022. However, my next question to Jenny is: "How will you feel about not having a mortgage? What will that mean to you?"

We talk around the idea for a few minutes until Jenny says, "It will make me feel more secure." This is when I encourage Jenny to examine her thinking. "Let's just make sure you understand where that's coming from," I say. "Will you really feel secure if you pay off your mortgage, or is this connected to your thinking around what security means? We want to make sure that, if you pay off your mortgage, this really is how you feel afterwards because, logically, you're right, it would make more financial sense to invest your money."

Deciding to pay off her mortgage is an emotional decision for Jenny, but that doesn't mean it's the wrong decision, If she pays off her mortgage and, one year from now, can sit in front of me and tell me that she has peace of mind because she knows she owns the roof over her head, this is the right decision for her. Of course, there are still plenty of things that could go wrong in Jenny's life, but this decision isn't about what those might be, it's about her thinking and where that decision will put her thinking.

When it comes to building true wealth, there is no cookie-cutter mindset to create. It is very much centred around what's important to you and making sure that your thinking allows you to see and evaluate solutions, rather than being fixated on problems.

Steve: rock bottom?

Steve ran a couple of pubs and restaurants. Business was going well, he was married with a son and life was good. Slowly, however, his personal life started to fall apart. He was working unsocial hours and therefore not able to spend as much time with his wife and son as he'd have liked, but he didn't redress the balance. Eventually, his wife asked for a divorce.

Steve felt like his world had crumbled. He didn't know what to do with himself. He didn't feel like he could face going to work and he locked himself in his apartment, sinking deeper and deeper into depression. "I'm at rock bottom," he told himself. "This is the worst situation in the world. I've got nothing to live for..." Of course, this wasn't true. He still had his son, he was fit and healthy and he had his businesses. But his perception was that things couldn't get any worse: until they did...

Having hidden away, it wasn't long before his businesses started struggling. He borrowed money to support them, then a little more, and he slipped further and further into debt and was facing bankruptcy. "This is rock bottom now, things really can't get any worse. This is the worst situation I've ever been in," Steve said. He was terrified of what being bankrupt would mean. Eventually the inevitable happened and he was declared bankrupt; this was when life started to change for Steve.

He realised that being bankrupt wasn't as bad as he'd believed. It was what he needed to hit the reset button. By this point, I was having conversations with him and doing what I could to help. I introduced him to a client of mine who ran a commercial cleaning company. Steve took an opportunity with this business and started to rebuild what he had lost.

Now, ten years down the road he has a very successful business employing around 75 people. He has circa £1 million in his pension pot; he's debt free and he has a great lifestyle that allows him to play golf and spend time with his son. If I had told him this would be the outcome when he was facing bankruptcy and was at his lowest point, he wouldn't have believed me. His thinking was so preoccupied with going bankrupt being the worst possible thing that he couldn't see any other opportunities or solutions.

However, once he became bankrupt he realised it wasn't as bad as he'd imagined and that's when his thinking started to change. He found there were endless opportunities around him if he could clear his mind enough to see them. All he had to do was improve his state of mind and improve his thinking around his situation to see that there were endless opportunities to improve his situation. Once he had that clarity, he was able to take one of those opportunities and build a better life than he ever thought possible.

A piece of the puzzle

The way you think is a very important piece of your real wealth puzzle, because it has such a significant impact on both your emotions and your behaviour. It might sound overly simplistic to say that you just need to change the way you think about a situation and things will improve, and while the concept might be simple, I know from experience that the shift itself can take time and effort to achieve.

That said, when you do change your thinking, solutions to your problems start to appear and you begin to see opportunities where previously you had only seen challenges. Sometimes you are so caught up on your own thinking that it takes someone external to help clear that fog of confusion. This is one of the reasons why working with a financial planner who you trust can be so valuable.

A good financial planner will encourage you to view your situation from other perspectives and in doing so will help you open up your thinking. As I explained at the start of this chapter, there are Three Principles to be aware of: Mind, Consciousness and Thinking. The more conscious you can be in every aspect of your life, the more clarity of thinking you will have and, therefore, the more opportunities and solutions you will find. Changing your thinking can also have an impact on the habits you choose to develop, which is what I'll cover in the following chapter.

You might be wondering why, if it's just as simple as changing your thinking, everyone doesn't do this and the answer is very simple: because we don't get told. Consider this your opportunity for a lightbulb moment. Switch your thinking and then look at any of the pieces of your puzzle you've been struggling to put together. Can you see a different way?

Chapter 5

FORMING GOOD HABITS AROUND MONEY

When you start forming good habits, you are making a commitment to change. It's important to recognise that forming good habits generally takes work and a change in your behaviour. Bad habits are the ones you can fall into easily. They are easier to maintain than good habits and that's why so many of us make New Year's resolutions only to have ditched them by the middle of January.

Breaking bad habits and forming good habits requires effort, takes time and most importantly that commitment to help you see them through. When you embark on a journey that will lead to forming good habits, there aren't any shortcuts. You have to show up every day and put in the work.

Think for just a moment about joining a gym. When you sign up to the gym, you're making a commitment to change. You know that you're going to need to go to the gym and workout at least a couple of times a week if you're going to get healthier and see your physical fitness improve. No one joins a gym and starts working out three times per week by accident. This routine, or habit, comes from commitment and a desire to reach a particular goal, whether that's training for an event or losing some weight.

The point is that you make a conscious decision to get fitter or healthier and only once you've made that decision do you start to explore the behaviours you need to exhibit to achieve that. In this example, you will need to join a gym and allocate time and be prepared to go. You also have to know your limitations – if you've never worked out before you're not going to go for a three-hour session at the gym from a standing start. You'll maybe start with just half an hour, then build up to an hour, try out the different machines and work out whether you enjoy it. This is when the habit starts to kick in and it's also when, if you are enjoying it, that you might decide you want to go to the gym more often or take your training more seriously.

Behaviours and habits will drive each other forward, but there isn't really an "end" to this process. If we take finances as an example, when someone reaches a point where financially they are very comfortable and they're very clear about what they need, they don't just stop there. They typically ask the question, "What do I want next?" Life, and the habits and behaviours we have in our lives, are an ever-evolving progression.

As I've said, good habits take work and reading this book on its own won't mean your life changes without you putting in any effort. However, what it will give you is a map and a narrative that allows you to see that what you really want is achievable. There are some steps you'll need to take along the way, but you can get help with them. You're not on your own and whatever challenges you face with breaking your bad habits and setting up good ones are not insurmountable.

Jake: laying the foundations for a strong financial future

Jake knows he's very fortunate to be where he is at this stage in his career. He's worked hard to break into a Premier League football side and now he's reaping the rewards, on and off the pitch. Although he's only in his 20s, he's got one eye on his future already.

He is well aware that while he's earning a very healthy wage at the moment, that could all change when his playing career comes to an end. With the potential for injury in every match, there's no telling when that might happen either. Hopefully he'll still be playing in his 30s, but you just never know.

His parents have given him good guidance around his money to this point, and with my support he's getting into great habits when it comes to investing for when he retires. He's laying the foundations for a strong financial future.

All too often we see footballers getting into financial trouble because they develop bad habits when they have an abundance of money. They get into the habit of spending more and more, but when their significant salary dries up at the end of their playing career, they don't change their behaviour. The habit of spending continues until they find themselves in serious financial difficulty. They haven't saved enough to support this lifestyle and they aren't even aware of how much "enough" is.

Developing unsustainable habits around money is a common issue, not only among Premier League footballers. It can be very hard to develop habits like saving regularly when you've been used to spending everything you earn (and often more, thanks to the likes of credit cards). The reason being that your mindset isn't in the right place. To change those kinds of habits, you have to get your mindset (your thinking) in the right place and only then can you start to change your behaviour to create more sustainable habits, like regularly saving money.

You also have to think about what habits authentically represent you as a person and your goals for your life and your future. Ask yourself whether you genuinely want what you're currently aiming for, because when you know that you genuinely want to achieve a particular goal you are much more likely to put in the work required to achieve it.

Finding your focus

We've all heard the flight attendant telling us to put our own oxygen mask on before helping others, and getting into good habits with our money is very similar. We have to make sure we're taking care of ourselves first and foremost. Only then can we turn our attention to everyone else in our lives.

But how do you do this in a way that's sustainable? This comes back to focusing on what you want for your life and lifestyle, and what value you place on that. Then you have to look at the means you have available to help achieve those goals. For example, you might decide homeownership is a goal of yours so you'll explore how you can save for a deposit. Or you may feel that homeownership is out of your reach because of the escalating costs, but you really want to travel so you look at how you can afford to go away two or three times a year.

If you make a list of everything you believe is important to you in your life and then compare this to the means you have available to achieve those things, you'll start to prioritise some elements over others and it will help you realise that some goals may not be as important to you as you imagined.

All too often, we fail to verbalise what we want our lives to look like and this means we don't make progress simply because we don't know where we should be going. Instead, we tread water and if something good happens, that's great, while if something bad happens we find a way to deal with it. However, what I've observed is that when people verbalise how they want their lives to be, it gives them the motivation they need to build good habits and change their behaviour. This, in turn, is what allows them to build wealth. They're taking control of their lives and the direction in which they're moving.

The key is to not only visualise the life that you want, but to also be realistic. It's no good visualising winning the EuroMillions because even if you buy tickets every week, you have no guarantee of ever winning anything. This isn't a financial or retirement plan based in reality. Being realistic is important because it means you can achieve milestones along the way and this will give you the drive to keep going with forming positive habits in your life.

It's also essential to be honest about where you currently are and how far you are from the life you want to be living. If you're not where you want to be, ask yourself what you can do to change it. What can you control? Can you apply for a new job, work longer or fewer hours, or cut back on your spending? You're deciding what you want your life to be and how your money can facilitate that to allow you to enjoy life, rather than spending all your time chasing money without knowing what you want to use that money for.

When you know what you need and want money for, it's much easier to change your behaviour accordingly and form the positive habits that will enable you to live the life you want.

Powerful positive habits

#1: Living within your means

One of the most powerful positive habits you can form when it comes to your finances is the habit of living within your means. By this I mean living off 80 per cent of your earnings and being able to put 20 per cent towards paying off your debt and saving into investments (more on this later). In the modern world, it's all too easy to take out a loan or credit card to pay for the next bright, shiny thing that you want. But all that happens when you do this is that you're getting your future to pay for your now.

There is nothing wrong with wanting things, or having goals and objectives that require you to spend money, but it's far better to get into the habit of saving for them before you buy them, rather than using debt to buy something you can't yet afford.

Connected to this habit of living within your means are a number of micro-habits that result in this behaviour. Among the most crucial are knowing where your money is and where it is being spent each month. Quite simply, this means having a budget that you review regularly and stick to. Use your budget to guide your spending, not just to track your outgoings. If you already have debt, it's important to understand how you can get out of it and to build the habit of paying off your debt.

For example, if you have credit card debt, it's best to pay off more than just the minimum amount you are asked for each month, as this will reduce the debt more quickly. A good tip is to come up with an amount that you are comfortable repaying each month (that is higher than the minimum due) and to pay that, rather than just the minimum, as it will help you clear your debt considerably faster and reduce the interest payments you accrue.

Compound interest works both ways. It's often cited as a great thing for accumulating money, but on the other side of the coin it also makes it easier to get further into debt. If you have debts, put a percentage of your income (usually 10–20 per cent) towards repaying these before you start saving money.

Saving regularly is another micro-habit that you can build that will help with the broader goal of living within your means.

The 80-10-10 approach

For many of us, the biggest debt we have is our mortgage. There's a really simple rule you can use for managing your money that will not only allow you to save a fortune in interest payments by paying off your mortgage early, but also enable you to put money into savings at the same time. This is the 80-10-10 approach.

The premise is simple: you live off 80 per cent of your salary. You use 10 per cent of what you earn each month to overpay on your mortgage (nearly every mortgage out there allows overpayments of up to 10 per cent per year without any additional charges). You put the final 10 per cent of your salary into savings.

The key to making this work is to automate these payments. For example, if you get paid on the 25th of the month, set up direct debits on the following day that will automatically put money into whatever savings or investment account you choose and into your mortgage account. Once you've set these payments up, you won't need to think about them again.

When it comes to getting into the habit of saving in particular, the key is to consider saving as a commitment rather than a luxury. All too often we tell ourselves that we'll start saving when we've paid off these bills, or when money is less tight, or when we get a pay rise... The problem is that you can't get this time back, so the longer you leave it to start saving, the more you will need to put away each month to achieve the same savings goals. Failing to save also increases the likelihood that you'll need to borrow money in the future, because you won't have built up financial resources over time.

As George S. Clason said in *The Richest Man In Babylon*: "A part of all you earn is yours to keep. It should be not less than a tenth no matter how little you earn. It can be as much more as you can afford. Pay yourself first."[10] Paying yourself can also refer to putting money into a pension, which is something that many business owners neglect.

#2: Living by your financial plan

If you look at many religions in the world, they encourage people to give money to support their local church/mosque/synagogue or whatever religious group you might believe in. In Christianity, for example, people are encouraged to give 10 per

---

10   Clason G.S., (1926), The Richest Man In Babylon, Penguin Books, page 14

cent of their wealth to the church. For many who follow this religion, this becomes a habit.

You don't have to give away a percentage of your wealth to a religious organisation to form this habit. However, the way in which religions view philanthropic giving can be applied to other situations in your life. The reason people give to religious organisations is because that act becomes inherently built into their moral code. You can use your financial plan as your own form of moral code that you follow, and provided that the goals you're working towards are inherently linked to your values, you'll form a strong enough attachment to them that you find it easier to form that habit of giving to yourself.

Creating your financial plan isn't a habit in itself, but regularly reviewing and updating this plan is a habit that is very useful to get into.

#3: Setting meaningful financial goals

Setting goals around your finances and, here's the key part, that are meaningful to you, will not only help you when you're creating your financial plan, but also when you're reviewing and updating it. When you're setting financial goals, think about how they align with your values. The more aligned they are with your values, the more likely you are to commit to achieving them.

As with your financial plan, it's also important that you regularly review these goals. Reminding yourself of the goals you're working towards can also be a good way to help you stay on track with your financial plan.

#4: Earning money while you sleep

If you've ever read the book *Rich Dad Poor Dad*[11] by Robert T. Kiyosaki, you'll likely be familiar with this concept. Essentially, this is about making passive income, one where you aren't having to exert effort to see a return. This could be in the form of rental income from a property or dividends you receive from a company you've invested in.

#5: Adding value

The habit of adding value can be particularly powerful, whether you're a business owner or employed. Think of it this way: the more value you add, the more you are likely to be paid and therefore the greater the positive impact on your future financial position and your general wellbeing. Simply focusing on the value you can deliver for your clients or to your employer is huge and will pay dividends in more ways than you might first imagine.

---

11   Robert T. Kiyosaki, (2017), Rich Dad Poor Dad: What the Rich Teach Their Kids About Money That the Poor and Middle Class Do Not!, Plata Publishing, Second edition

#6: Giving

I talked earlier about the habit of giving that is ingrained in many religions, but there is a lot to be said for giving away some of what you earn, if you can afford to. There's the old adage that "givers gain" and it's important to think about how we can help others by giving away some of our earnings on a regular basis.

You can derive a great deal of enjoyment from giving your money away and seeing how it helps other people and does good in the world.

#7: Protecting your assets

This is about getting into the habit of having the right insurance in place to protect your greatest money-making machine, you. All too often, people don't value life insurance, yet will happily pay for insurance for their physical belongings. Think now about what you'd do if you had a machine in your back garden that churned out money, day in, day out. Would you pay to have insurance for that in case it broke down or got stolen? Of course you would!

However, in life you are this money-making machine. This is why it's so important to make sure you're insured to an adequate level. Don't get me wrong, there is plenty of un-useful insurance in the world, but there are certain types of insurance that are very useful indeed and it's these that you need to consider when it comes to protecting your assets (which include you!).

I would argue that insuring your life and your health is far more important than insuring your mobile phone or your fridge-freezer.

Protecting your assets also stretches to protecting your wealth by taking steps like paying off your credit cards in full each month.

#8: Understanding your priorities

Value can be quite an intangible concept, especially when you think of your possessions that may not have a high resale value, even though they mean a lot to you. Knowing where your priorities lie will help you see where you are, perhaps, prepared to spend a little more and where you could spend a little less.

For example, Simon told me he spent £15 on a pair of socks for his granddaughter for Christmas. They were the socks from the latest Aston Villa kit. He said, "I wouldn't spend £15 on a pair of socks for myself, but I'm prepared to spend that for her because I want her to be happy. That's what's important to me."

There's a simple exercise you can do to see where you're placing your priorities. Go through your wardrobe and tally up how much you've spent on the contents (roughly). Then consider how much of what's in your wardrobe rarely sees the light of day.

I'm not saying you shouldn't spend money on these things if it's within your means and you can, but just understand that there is a consequence to spending money here in that it won't be going somewhere else that could better align with your priorities and values in life.

If, however, you realise that you're chasing material possessions to the detriment of other aspects of your life and financial plan, consider what changes you can make to redress the balance.

#9: Educating yourself and others

Continuing to educate yourself doesn't only have a positive effect on your financial wellbeing, but also your wellbeing in general. I particularly like the concept of "sharpen the saw", which is referred to in Stephen R. Covey's book *The 7 Habits of Highly Effective People*[12]. This refers to the process of continual education and how this benefits you in a multitude of ways.

There are many ways you can educate yourself, from reading books to seeking out mentors. The latter can be particularly beneficial in a business context. The key, whether you are looking for education in a business or personal context, is to be willing to learn and open to new perspectives.

---

12   Stephen R. Covey, (2020), The 7 Habits of Highly Effective People, Simon & Schuster, Revised and updated 30th anniversary edition

This idea of education is important for the next generation, too. In the UK, our financial education is seriously lacking. We don't offer any kind of formal financial education to children and this means that they often learn about money and wealth from less-than-ideal avenues. One example that springs to mind comes from Simon, whose grandson loves watching YouTube videos of people getting given thousands of dollars for doing stupid pranks. He doesn't understand that this money comes from advertising revenue, all he sees is someone doing something silly and getting paid money.

Similarly, young people are encouraged to spend money in the games they play to get something that will give them an advantage. The endorphin hit they get from spending that money and "using" their purchase will last minutes at best, in many cases only seconds. There is no realisation of value in these transactions and this is what many young people are exposed to on an almost daily basis via social media, games and other avenues.

My point here is that you can't rely on other people to educate your children or others around you when it comes to finances. You have to take responsibility for educating the people who rely on you and who look to you for support. This is also a good opportunity to check in with your own behaviour around money and assess whether you're in a strong enough position to look after the interests of the next generation. If not, this can act as motivation to develop better habits around money yourself, which you can in turn pass on.

#10: Thinking before you spend

Where debt is concerned, people often talk about "good debt" and "bad debt". However, the distinction isn't so much related to good and bad, but to what you get out of taking on that debt. For example, a mortgage would be classed as "good" debt, because it allows you to buy a home that will more than likely appreciate in value. Another example that falls into the "good" debt category could be borrowing money to enable you to start a business.

"Bad" debt, meanwhile, will enable you to purchase something that will depreciate in value. Credit cards and loans are usually the types of debt used for purchases of this nature, both of which typically have higher interest rates than the likes of a mortgage. If you're thinking of buying something on credit, pause before you hit the "buy now" button. Ask yourself whether it's essential or discretionary; whether you really need it, and whether you really want it. Developing your consciousness around spending and noticing when you are going to get into debt to make a purchase enables you to question your spending habits. If you currently find that you make impulse buys and overspend, it's also a very useful way of checking and changing that behaviour.

A top tip is to wait at least 24 hours before making a purchasing decision. Use that time to think about whether what you're about to spend money on is something you really need and want. If the answer is that you don't really need or want what you're about to buy, you can evaluate and change your decision, saving you money in the process. It's the simple change to your behaviour of waiting 24 hours to make a purchase that will help prevent you spending money unnecessarily.

A piece of the puzzle

Forming new habits requires us to change our behaviour and this is much easier to do if you understand what motivates your behaviour in the first place. This is why checking in on your thinking, as I discussed earlier, is so important because it will help you to understand what drives certain financial decisions.

The habits I've shared in this chapter are ones that I know can help improve people's lives. Which ones you would benefit from adopting, however, will depend on your circumstances and what you want to achieve. When you have identified your overall goal and know what your desired lifestyle looks like, it will motivate you to make some of the potentially more challenging behavioural shifts, because you will understand how it will benefit you in the future.

Chapter 6

GETTING IT OUT ON THE TABLE

By this stage, you will hopefully have a clearer idea of what the picture of your jigsaw puzzle looks like. You'll be at least starting to think about your values, what's important to you in your life and what goals you want to work towards. When you reach this point, you have to get practical. This is a bit like laying out all the pieces of your jigsaw puzzle before you start piecing it together. You're assessing what you have and looking to see whether there are any important parts that are missing.

How full is your wealth bucket?

If you're working with a financial planner, part of the discovery process will involve working out exactly which pieces of your puzzle you have already and whether they are contributing to, or draining, your wealth bucket. This will begin with the money you have available that you can get your hands on now: your

ISAs, current accounts, savings accounts and possibly some shares or National Savings. This is your liquidity and it's the water that is poured into your bucket.

Once you know what liquid assets you have available, you turn your attention to the other elements that you need to be aware of. Most people consider their home to be an asset, for example, but this is actually a liability rather than an asset and, as such, it doesn't add liquid to your bucket. The reason it's a liability is that you'll likely be paying a mortgage, and you'll certainly be paying your bills, council tax, upkeep and so on. This means it's draining funds from your bucket. However, your property can contribute to what's in your bucket if, for example, you sell it, downsize and transfer some of the money you make from the sale into your pool of liquid assets.

Another way to look at it, as Simon explains, is that your property is an asset for your dependents and beneficiaries, but it's a lifestyle expense during your lifetime. "We've all heard stories about mega-rich people who have had to sell their properties and downsize. It's not that their homes aren't worth money, it's just that if they want to carry on living in them, they have to spend money to maintain them. The bigger your house, the larger your bills; and it's not until you actually liquidate it that you can say what it's worth is 'your money'. Your home is effectively a lifestyle expenditure choice." Of course, not all properties are a liability. If you have multiple properties that you rent out, these would be producing a positive cash flow and therefore contributing liquid to your bucket, rather than draining your resources.

Another element to consider is your pension, which also sits outside of your wealth bucket because you can't access this money until you're 55 (going forward this will increase to 57), while your State Pension won't be accessible to you until you're in your late 60s at the earliest (depending on how old you are now). When you do access your private pension, 25 per cent of it will be paid to you and therefore contribute to the liquid in your bucket, but the remainder will be paid to you as an income over time.

Similar to owning a property, you might also own a business. This, too, is a liability. You want to plan for financial independence from your business, but a lot of people consider their business to be their pension. While we can plan for this to be the case, we also have to consider what might happen if there is no market for your business in the future. We will explore what will happen if there is a sale in the future, but at the present time it's more likely that you'll simply have some profits, a salary and maybe dividends coming in from the business and topping up your wealth bucket.

Another element to consider for the future is any inheritance you expect to receive. Again, this is important to be aware of, but we can't add that amount to your wealth bucket at this stage because you don't have the inheritance right now. By the time we have explored each of these aspects of your finances, we'll have a good idea of what exactly is going into your bucket, so the next step is to look at what's going out.

What's draining your wealth bucket?

Imagine there's a tap at the bottom of the bucket, which is where your current lifestyle expenses are drawn from. These expenses cover everything from your bill payments and children's school fees to holidays you take each year.

This is particularly important because, in my experience, most people don't have a handle on what's going out of their accounts each month, even if they have a good idea of how much is going in. The truth is that the vast majority of people don't keep too close an eye on what's going out as long as they aren't getting letters or phone calls telling them that they're overdrawn. Therefore it's really important to document your expenditure in detail so that you can identify any leaks you might have in your wealth bucket.

The idea is that, if you've got £5,000 a month coming into your account, you should be able to account for every penny of that somehow. I have met many clients earning a similar amount to this who will tell me that their bills and expenses each month amount to £2,500, yet when I ask them how much they have in savings the answer is "£10,000-£20,000". If you've been working for 20 years and not spending £2,500 a month, you should have £500,000 in savings! But people don't pay attention to where the rest of their money goes as long as they are broadly financially comfortable.

For example, if you smoke 20 cigarettes a day, at £8 per pack that's an expense of £56 per week, or £220 per month. That adds up to a sizable amount over the course of a year. Similarly, if you're buying takeaway coffees every day, that adds up to hundreds of pounds each month. American financial planner David Bach calls this "the latte factor" in his book of the same name[13]. Now, he's not talking about spending money on coffee per se, but about considering this expenditure in the context of what's important to you in life. If you're spending £5 every day on your way to work buying a coffee and a pastry, that's £25 per week, or £100 per month. If that's important to you and you enjoy it, you don't have to give it up, but do consider how this is affecting your future financial wellbeing.

---

13   David Bach and John David Mann, (2019), The Latte Factor: Why You Don't Have to Be Rich to Live Rich, Atria Books, illustrated edition

This exercise, where you examine exactly what is pouring out of your wealth bucket each month, is about distinguishing your essential expenditure (which should be drained from the tap) and your discretionary expenditure (which is leaking out of the tap because you're not turning it off properly). Discretionary expenditure can fall under the umbrella of convenience, luxury, social or lifestyle. That isn't actually what's important; what you have to decide is whether what you're spending is worth it for what you're getting out of the transaction. It's a cost-value analysis.

What's Going To Happen To YOUR Bucket?

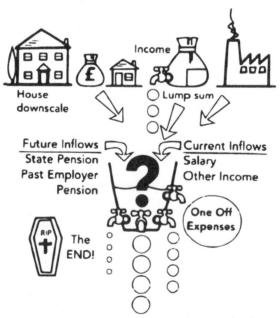

Thank you to Paul Armson for the use of this diagram

Mike: plugging the leaks

Mike, a senior executive at a large UK business, was a classic example of the kind of person who had a fair idea of what was going into his bank account each month, but very little visibility over what was going out. Ahead of his first meeting with me, I introduced him to the wealth bucket concept and asked him to complete the exercise of listing his incomings and outgoings each month.

At our meeting, I asked Mike how he'd found the exercise. "Honestly," he said, "I found it incredibly useful. I cancelled my gym membership, I've reduced my Sky subscription and I've cut expenses in a few other places. I'm already four grand a year better off!"

That cost saving more than paid for the time he was spending with me, not to mention that these are savings he'll continue to make year in, year out. Plugging the leaks in your wealth bucket is very worthwhile.

If you think about it, no matter how much you're earning there are probably places where you can reduce your expenditure. How many times have you signed up for a service to get it free for a few months, only to forget about it and see it renew? Do you even notice when this happens? Now that banking is carried out online and through apps, many of us simply fail to take the time to look at what's going out of our accounts each month. We approach our money differently now that we don't receive paper statements and bills in the post.

What you also have to remember is that, even if you're only paying a small amount each month, it all adds up – £8 per month for a music streaming service, for example, adds up to almost £100 per year. You only need to cancel three or four payments like that, and you've saved £400 straightaway.

You have to notice the drips to stop them

The key is to be aware of what you are spending money on each month. Technology has made it increasingly easy for us, and for other members of our family, to spend money. Smart speakers are a classic example. For instance, you can have a subscription to a music streaming service at a basic level, but if you want to play different songs in different rooms at the same time, you need to upgrade to the next level of subscription, more than doubling the price from £7 a month to £14.99 a month.

If you have a smart speaker and more than one person wants to listen to different music at the same time, the smart speaker will ask, "Would you like to upgrade your subscription?" All you have to say is, "Yes" and all of a sudden you're paying £14.99 instead of £7. Now, the smart speaker doesn't distinguish between children and adults, so your kids could upgrade your subscription and unless you check your payments, you may not notice. Simon reveals this has happened to him, "I once found out I'd had two months of paying for unlimited music because my grandchildren had agreed to the upgrade!"

His experience wasn't overly costly, but I'm sure you've heard the stories about children playing computer games who run up bills of thousands of pounds making in-game purchases. The point is that all of these microtransactions add up and if you don't keep an eye on them, they can drain a substantial amount from your wealth bucket.

Tax is another drain on your wealth bucket. Of course, paying tax is a good sign, because it means you are doing well. However, it's important to make sure you're not paying too much tax and that you're utilising the government legislation to make the most of your allowances and legally reduce your tax bill. It's very important to stress that tax evasion is illegal, but there is nothing wrong with using all of your allowances to keep more of your money in your wealth bucket and see less of it drain away in taxation.

You will find an exercise you can complete to get an overview of your expenditure by scanning the QR code.

SCAN ME

How much do you need in your wealth bucket?

It's all well and good making sure that you keep your wealth bucket topped up and that you stop the leaks where you can, but it's just as important to know how much you need in your wealth bucket to not only maintain your current lifestyle, but also for your desired future lifestyle.

The next stage in this exercise is therefore to make a list of what you would like to do more of in the future and how this will make your life and your expenditure look different. What you're doing here is looking at how much you need to have in your wealth bucket to turn that desired lifestyle from a pipe dream into a reality. This will show you what the gap is between where you are currently and your desired lifestyle.

In my experience, people typically fall into one of three camps, as described in Paul Armson's book *Enough?*[14]:

1. **The not enoughs:** These people won't have enough for their desired lifestyle if they continue the way they are. They will benefit the most from going through this process and taking action based on what they discover to help them close the gap between their reality and desired lifestyle.

2. **The probably okays:** These people will probably be OK and achieve their desired lifestyle, but at this point they don't know this is the case. By completing this exercise, they will gain peace of mind that they are on track, or know what they need to do to catch up. In some cases, this process may allow them to see how they could achieve their desired lifestyle more quickly.

3. **The definitely have enough alreadys:** These people have more than enough for their desired lifestyle already. Their problem is not a lack of resources, but the fact that they aren't living their desired lifestyle even though they could be. This exercise will help these people gain clarity over the strength of their financial situation and (hopefully)

---

14   Armson P, (2016), Enough?: How Much Money Do You Need For The Rest of Your Life?, CreateSpace Independent Publishing Platform, first edition

encourage them to spend more and live the life they want now, rather than waiting for an arbitrary date in the future. This is all about being the best version of yourself and living the life that you want and that you've worked hard to build.

When you are calculating how much you need in your metaphorical bucket, it's also important to consider one-off expenses, such as money towards a child's wedding, travelling for six months, providing a deposit for a property for your child, paying off your mortgage, or maybe even settling a divorce in the near future. These are potentially large expenses, but they will only be coming out of your bucket once. You still need to account for them when you're planning your future cash flow, though, to ensure that there is enough left in your bucket for you to continue living your desired lifestyle.

Don't forget later life costs

While we may not always like to talk about it, it's important to remember that as we get older we may need to pay for medical treatment or care. The key is to balance living your ideal lifestyle with planning to ensure you have enough to support you should you be in a position where you need to start paying for care, for instance. While I'm a big advocate of living life to the full, you also need to make sure you don't spend everything and leave yourself in an uncomfortable position in your later years.

Using cash flow planning, I can help my clients see what those costs might be in the future and therefore how much they need to leave in reserve in case they need it. This can help ensure they are able to maintain a comfortable lifestyle in later life, where they have a choice over where they live and who provides their care, rather than relying on the state to make provisions.

Planning your finances in this way gives you peace of mind that you will have resources to support you if you do fall ill or your health deteriorates.

Consider inheritance tax in relation to your wealth bucket

At the time of writing in the UK, if you are fortunate enough to have built up a sizable financial position in excess of £1 million, you will have a 40 per cent "exit fee" when you pass away, in the form of inheritance tax. You might be happy for that money to go to the Treasury, but it's important that I have this conversation with you and make you aware of your inheritance tax position. Other people are keen to do whatever they can to ensure as little of their money as possible goes to HMRC.

Whichever camp you fall into, it's important to be aware of your inheritance tax position and to plan accordingly.

There are some very high-profile celebrities who have publicly said that they don't intend to leave their vast fortunes to their children. However, that doesn't mean they're handing it all over to HMRC. Instead they will plan the legacies they are going to leave, make donations and so on. For those who do want to leave an inheritance for their children, it's important to plan this carefully so that what they receive isn't devastated by a significant tax bill when the time comes. Within the UK, there are various, perfectly legal, mechanisms you can use to reduce your inheritance tax liability and ensure that more of your wealth passes to the people or organisations you want to benefit from it.

This is particularly relevant if you fall into the "definitely have enough already" camp, as you will never get through your wealth in your lifetime. Therefore, you need to carefully consider what you want to happen to what remains when you pass away and plan for that now, rather than waiting.

The wealth bucket: bringing clarity to your financial position

The point of this exercise, which is a comprehensive audit of your finances, is to give you clarity over where you are and where you're heading. When I work through this process with my clients, my overarching aim is to give them the clarity they currently lack around their money and what their future looks like from a financial perspective. Once they have gained this clarity, it is much easier for them to grasp the importance of planning, which supports all the steps we then take as part of this process.

Once a client has shared their goals, objectives, income, assets, liabilities and financial position with me, I can model what the future might look like. We can assess whether that future is one the client is happy with or whether they need to change direction. The beauty of carrying out an exercise like this earlier in your life is that you will have the power to do something about it and change the course you're on if you don't like the look of the future you're building.

This clarity and knowledge that, no matter what happens you will probably be okay financially, is also incredibly empowering.

It comes back to what I was talking about earlier, in terms of trying to piece together your jigsaw puzzle without being able to see what the picture should look like. Most people have gathered some of the pieces – they've got a mortgage, insurance, a pension, debt and so on – but what they lack is clarity about the picture they're trying to put together. They can't see how the different pieces connect and they aren't sure what they are missing to bridge that gap.

What allows you to see the picture you're trying to piece together is having a financial plan. Working out what's going into and out of your wealth bucket is the first essential step towards creating a detailed financial plan. Whenever I work with a new client, I always ask them to bring a copy of their most up-to-date financial plan to their first meeting, which is a request that's usually met with silence. However, your financial plan is the foundation for your financial future. Without it you're flying blind.

It's a lot like rushing out to buy the furniture for the home of your dreams before you've bought the land you're going to build on and engaged an architect to design it. You wouldn't jump to buying furniture before you've completed those two steps. In fact, the first step would likely be hiring an architect, sharing your vision of your dream home and working closely with them to draw up the plans. That is exactly what I do, as a financial planner. When you share the vision of your desired lifestyle, I can create a plan that will help you get there, or show you that you're closer than you might think to realising your dreams.

This practical stage, where you look at your wealth bucket and analyse both its contents and leaks, needs to follow the work you've already done around identifying your values, your purpose and what's truly important to you in life.

Of course, there might be instances when someone comes to me and their current financial position is incompatible with their desired lifestyle because they have unrealistic goals. Even if that's the case, they still gain a lot from having that clarity about their financial situation. In gaining this clarity, it can also help them to evaluate what they want from their lives and create a new, more appropriate desired lifestyle and therefore a realistic and achievable financial plan.

A piece of the puzzle

The practical steps of working out what's pouring into and what's draining out of your wealth bucket allow you to have a clear picture of where you are right now. When you know where you are starting from, it makes it much easier to work out what your next steps need to be, both in the short and long term.

The wealth bucket exercise might take some time and effort on your part, but it is more than worth it – just look at Mike's story, and he is far from the only client I've worked with who has saved substantial sums of money each month just by becoming more aware of where their money is being spent.

Once you have this clarity about where you stand in the present, you can begin to plan your future with greater confidence and certainty.

Part 3

SHAPING THE FUTURE

In this final part of the book, I'm going to look at how having a financial plan and working with a financial planner can help you shape your future. I'll begin by looking at the practical side of implementing your financial plan, explaining what a financial plan looks like and how I go about creating one with my clients.

It's important to remember that financial plans constantly evolve, both as your life and the world around you changes. However, having a plan in place can give you incredible peace of mind and bring a degree of certainty to much of the uncertainty we have about the future. A financial plan won't end with you either, as it will also consider your legacy.

Talking about how you want not only your financial wealth, but also your values, experiences and purpose to be passed onto your loved ones when you pass away is essential for helping you leave a legacy that can last for generations. I'll share the story of the Vanderbilt and Rothschild families to illustrate just how vital it is to consider your legacy and why it's beneficial to do so sooner rather than later.

In the final two chapters of the book, I'll seek to dispel some of the misconceptions about how much of your financial planning you can effectively complete on your own, and highlight the many advantages of working with both a financial planner and a wider team of professionals who can support every aspect of your plan and therefore give you stronger foundations on which to build your future.

Working closely and developing long-term relationships with a financial planner who understands you, your values, your goals and aspirations, as well as the meaning of true wealth, will make all the difference. They will support you not only in terms of ensuring you are in a financially strong position, but also in terms of helping you live the life you want. I'm talking about a life that embodies true wealth, where you are fulfilled and living a life aligned with your values and purpose.

Chapter 7

IMPLEMENTING A PLAN

In Chapter 6 we looked at all the information you need to gather in order to create a comprehensive and valuable financial plan. When I have this information from a client, I can input everything into a financial planning tool.This allows me to go beyond assessing someone's current position and instead see how their finances may look in the future.

I can run numerous scenarios through this financial planning tool, making different assumptions each time to see how life or economic events could affect that individual client's future. For example, I can map the effect of assumed interest rate growth and inflation on savings, or I can look at what paying off a mortgage might mean for your finances in 15 years time.

The beauty of this kind of financial planning software is that, once you've input all the data, you are able to roll forward, year by year, to see what your future financial position could look like. In doing so, we're building up the pieces of the jigsaw puzzle that you have available and we're bringing much more clarity to the picture you're creating.

By the time you're creating your financial plan, you know what your ideal lifestyle is and what you are aiming for. This process allows you to see how far away you are from achieving that and what you may need to change to get there more quickly.

It can also highlight potential issues with your current strategy that you will then be able to address. For example, if much of your wealth is tied up in property then on paper you may have a lot of money but you have to consider how you are going to access that capital when you need it. Identifying this as a potential future issue when you are in your 40s, for instance, will give you time to adjust your strategy to ensure you have access to the funds you need as you get older.

Creating your detailed financial plan is all about making sure, first and foremost, that you have enough and then exploring whether it's in the right place, fit for purpose, and ties in with your values and what you've told me about how you want to live your life in the future.

This process doesn't only involve looking at your money and your assets, but also what products you have. This might be insurance policies, to make sure you're sufficiently covered, or investment products, to ensure your money is being managed in the most tax-efficient way. If you're a higher-rate tax payer, this is particularly important and even if you have more than enough, you still don't want to be paying more tax than is necessary.

Your financial time machine

The analogy I often use with clients when we work through this process is that we're jumping in the TARDIS and we're going to go 20 or 30 years into the future to see what that looks like, based on their current resources and what they've told me they want to achieve. If you don't like what you see when you get out of the TARDIS, we just jump back in, come back to the present and explore what we can do to improve or change that future. This is a highly interactive process and I work through different scenarios with my clients, showing them what I see in my "crystal ball".

One of the main aims of this process is to connect your goals with your timeline and life events. What I create with financial planning tools is a snapshot of what the future could be. The aim of this exercise is to give you some clarity about where you are and where you are heading. You wouldn't sail across the Atlantic from Southampton to New York without checking you were on the right course periodically, and running these scenarios through financial planning tools is really no different. It's an opportunity to check in and make sure you're still on course for where you want to head. What comes out of this financial planning meeting is a roadmap, with the major life events you've identified as being important to you, plotted out along the way.

As Simon explains, even if the road you're travelling on is broadly the same, the journey can be very different each time. "My wife's family come from Glasgow, so I've spent years driving from the Midlands to Scotland and the distance we travel is always the same, but the length of time it takes can vary considerably! The time it takes to do that drive is affected by so many variables. I remember when we first used to do the drive and it was just the two of us, it would usually take about five and a half hours with a stop for something to eat. But the best time I ever managed it was four and a half hours, because my wife was asleep, I didn't have to stop once and the roads were really clear." However, when they had children their journeys changed.

"Once the kids came along and we had a dog, we had to stop more. Then there was a period of time when there were a lot of roadworks on the route. All that meant that, on average, our journeys to Scotland would take six to seven hours, although on some occasions it's taken us as long as ten hours!" Simon notes. How does this relate to your financial roadmap? You know what you want to achieve, so the destination will remain broadly the same (Scotland) but with the financial planning tool you can see how different circumstances and conditions might affect your journey.

What you don't want to do is take the best-case scenario (a four-and-a-half-hour drive to Scotland) and assume that it will always be like that. Equally, you don't want to work on the assumption that it will always take you ten hours to complete that drive. This tool allows us to see what both scenarios look like (as well as others in the middle) and to explore what we can do to improve your "driving conditions" to minimise the chances of you having those ten-hour drives.

This might be looking at what would happen if you saved more of your disposable income in your pension, or it could be exploring why you've decided to work to 65 when you have the means to stop working when you're 58.

What can you predict?

When it comes to creating your financial plan, the main assumptions I work with are your income and your capability to produce more income – either from your resources, your business or career – and your expenditure (which is why the wealth bucket exercise from Chapter 6 is so important).

Expenditure has a significant impact on how your roadmap plays out, which is why it's so important to be honest about your spending habits and to know exactly where all of your money goes each month. If I'm sitting with a client who is telling me they have £20,000 a year spare, I want to know where that is being saved! As I explained in the last chapter, if you don't know where your money goes, it will more than likely be leaking out of your wealth bucket.

As I previously mentioned, creating a detailed financial plan isn't only about your money and assets, it's also about planning for those big life events that can impact your financial position and either enhance or negatively affect your overall wellbeing. Using a financial planning tool, I can plot those on your timeline to show you how they might affect your finances, either positively or negatively. This can include everything from receiving an inheritance or selling your business to getting divorced or paying for your children to go to university.

Throughout this planning meeting, I ask my client to tell me what assumptions they'd like to test and to explore what level of risk they're willing to take in order to achieve their goals. Together, we can answer all the "what if?" questions they might have about their future and how it could look from a financial – but also a lifestyle – perspective. If, along the way, we identify any potential issues, we can explore solutions together.

Of course, we can't predict everything and there are no guarantees, particularly when we're forecasting a long way into the future. But, much like the drive to Glasgow that Simon talked about, we can predict certain things with a degree of certainty. If you were planning a drive, you could look at what roadworks were scheduled, or perhaps big events happening at key places along the way, and plan your route accordingly. If you're driving to Glasgow this Saturday, you can check the weather forecast. If, however, you're planning to drive to Glasgow five years from now, you won't have any certainty over the weather or the roadwork schedule, but based on what you know about the route you can still plan the drive, just with a lesser degree of certainty over how long it will take.

Financial plans constantly evolve

This is a key point, because, as I've explained and I'm sure you're aware, things can change. This means the assumptions we make today may not still be accurate a year from now, or five years from now. This is why it's so important to have regular meetings (I usually recommend once a year) to assess your plan, make sure you are still on track and to check that the assumptions we made last time we met are still accurate and appropriate for your situation.

These regular meetings are also an opportunity for you to check that the financial goals you're working towards are still what you want and, if not, to explore what you want to aim for instead.

It's also important to keep assessing the level of risk associated with your investments to make sure this is acceptable to you in terms of the return they deliver and also the risk to your capital. If you have enough to live comfortably for the rest of your life without needing to rely on an income from your investments, there is no sense in having these in high-risk products, for example. Similarly, it's important to consider what might happen in financial markets and whether any of your investments could become more risky over time. The petrochemical industry is a good example of one that could become less attractive due to changes in legislation relating to the climate crisis, for instance.

I will also encourage you to question your investments in relation to your values, to ensure that what you are putting your hard-earned money into is congruent with your values and the way you live your life.

Factoring in your business

If you're an entrepreneur with a business, this will play an important role in your financial planning. One of the areas I focus on with entrepreneurs is how their business contributes to their personal financial plan. As an example, if we work out that you need to save £20,000 a year, our next step will be to look at your business to see how we could use the business as a vehicle to achieve that in a tax-efficient way.

For instance, we could look at how feasible it would be for your business to increase its profitability by two per cent per year and, if that happens, how your business could pay that two per cent into your pension. If you see your business as your pension, it's also important to discuss how much you need in your business to have enough and also to consider what could happen if your business doesn't perform as expected or if the market changes.

What I encourage my clients to do, rather than relying solely on their business to provide a pension, is to plan to use their business to contribute more to their personal balance sheet over time. This is a much more sensible approach and more reliable than pinning your financial future on the eventual sale of your business. Of course, if you're only a year or two away from exiting, we can factor this in, but if you have five, ten, or more years until you intend to sell your business, it's too risky to assume that it will provide the sum you're hoping for as there are too many variables that could affect its value, both positively and negatively.

As with your personal financial plan, I can take all the data you have about your business, as well as a range of assumptions, and run it through my financial planning tool to see how different scenarios could play out.

Instead, it's better to create a financial plan that takes care of your goals and that uses your business as a bonus when the time comes. This also leads into the conversation about what you want to happen to your business in the future: do you want to sell it, do you want to pass it to someone else in your family, or do you want to liquidate it?

This brings us into a conversation around legacy, which I'll talk more about in the next chapter. When it comes to business succession, it's important to ensure your business is independent of you and that you have someone in the business who is capable of taking on its running.

Steve and Gemma: the benefits of an evolving plan

I've known Steve for so long I genuinely can't remember when we first met, but having worked with many members of his family and his in-laws it seemed almost inevitable we would work together to help him plan his financial future. However, unlike most of his family, Steve lived in the North of England

and commuting from there to Birmingham (where I'm based) seemed less than ideal; so, without much fanfare and no hard feelings, he felt he would be better served by someone more local to him.

We stayed in touch over the years and he informed me he'd regularly been sorting out his finances and was in a good place. Unbeknown to me, however, Steve was discussing his experience with some of his family members who were my clients, and wondered why he felt more confused than they did about where they were going financially, and why he seemed to be paying more tax.

He was managing director of his family construction business, which had incorporated in 2005. The business was successful and both he and his sister were the principal shareholders with 75 per cent and 25 per cent respectively. Steve knew eventually he wanted to build a company that he could pass on to his children, but given at the time his eldest child was seven, the second six and the youngest three, this all seemed a long time off.

In 2018, we decided to meet up to have a "chat" about his position. He told me he wanted to start planning for financial independence at the age of 55.

Importantly, the first thing I asked him wasn't what he had, or how much he was worth, but what he wanted to achieve during his lifetime, what success would look like to him, how much would be enough to deliver him the life he wanted, whether he had enough now and what he wanted to have happen to his wealth when he no longer needed it, as well as how long he would like his wealth to last for his children and any descendants.

Steve was a little surprised as he hadn't really given much thought to many of these questions. Instead he had spent most of the previous five years adding to his pension that had been set up to receive payments from his company. It was definitely tax efficient and the plans delivered one of his desired objectives, but really not much else. He'd acquired a few protection plans, including a joint life first death whole of life plan for tax planning, but wasn't really sure why.

By discussing his values and life goals I was able to understand what was really important to him and get a good grasp of his expected timeline. We agreed that I would complete a full audit on his finances, both personal and business, involve his wife Gemma and agree their priorities.

At our next meeting, having undertaken the work promised, I was able to deliver a one-page plan, which may have been light on product recommendations but clearly detailed what was important to Steve and Gemma – as well as any potential dangers that existed, their personal goals and objectives for life (not their money), potential strategies that could be suitable and actions that should be taken. This was designed to help reduce his stress and give him peace of mind.

With this information, Steve agreed that rather than focus on which pension might be best or how much to contribute, actually stepping back and looking at all the pieces of his financial jigsaw would be more effective than what he had been doing.

I put together a financial plan for Steve and Gemma, and built in potential "what if?" scenarios to illustrate how actions taken now could impact their future. This cash flow modelling allowed them both to see into their potential future and visualise how their actions now could have repercussions on the life they wanted to have.

Whilst I don't focus on products, suddenly Steve and Gemma were making contributions not only to a pension for him, but for them both, utilising other tax-efficient solutions where necessary and also making sure that there were written plans in place for them personally and for the business.

We reviewed their protection planning – as they now appreciated and understood that having money isn't always the same as protecting that wealth should circumstances change – and we established a regular ongoing review process.

Change is inevitable, which is why ongoing reviews are vital to weather the ups and downs that life throws at you. The pandemic in 2020 could have impacted some of their plans, particularly as they were in construction and sites around the country were suddenly closed, but they were not concerned as we had factored in the effects of a market decline or loss of income. As it turned out, while unexpected and unprecedented in modern times, the pandemic was a bump not a catastrophe.

Strangely enough, the time provided Steve with an opportunity to explore how he might exit his business, which we thought would still be ten years away, and look at a proposal to consider the use of an Employee Ownership Trust. This accelerated his plans significantly, and happily I was there to help, albeit in a more limited capacity.

Steve is still working in the family business, and will continue to do so for at least the next eight years. However, rather than him being the main shareholder, the company is now run by the Trust. He remains the managing director and still has shares, but he has managed to extract – both from cash reserves and future income – a very generous sale price that is being paid to his personal estate.

This has generated some new topics of discussion, but again the use of planning is effective when dealing with changes and has resulted in broader investment solutions to provide additional diversification, resilience and tax efficiency.

We have started making provision for estate planning and, although a tax liability would potentially exist if Steve and Gemma had passed away last week, they know how much this would be and where it could be paid from. We have started placing money into trust for the benefit of the family and future generations, as well as protecting the liability that the company carries should Steve or his sister no longer be around to manage the transition.

Estate and legacy planning was something Steve and Gemma were initially willing to put off until the future. Most of their collective wealth was in the business, which had exemptions, but this change and the relationship we have built has allowed them to appreciate that planning effectively means taking action and making conscious decisions.

Steve wants to pass wealth to his family. Knowing how much will be enough for his own lifetime and how much he can afford to give away means that he can pass money with a warm hand, not a cold one, and be around to see it happen.

There isn't an end to this journey that I can comment upon here as we are all still relatively young and this planning will be in place far longer than I am. It is a story that I know Steve and Gemma share with their family and friends, and they have become advocates for the way in which I help my clients and for that I am very proud of the service I deliver.

What does a financial plan look like?

The following is an example of a one-page financial plan that I produce for my clients. Having completed an in-depth analysis and cash flow forecast, including various "what if" scenarios that are tied to their life events, goals and objectives, I then produce this document in order to create a simple actionable plan.

As I've explained, the data I feed into the cash flow modelling software is important, but a good financial plan is not all about the data. This process is bookended by open and honest conversations about what you want to achieve in your life, what your values are and how you can use your money to support your overall wellbeing.

PROVEST
WEALTH MANAGEMENT

YOUR ONE-PAGE FINANCIAL PLAN

This plan is prepared for	Joe & Jane Bloggs
By	Paul Tracey
Date	25/01/2023

Your Values and What is Important to You	Meaning and purpose
	Independence and security
	Ensuring that we can maintain our lifestyle now and later in life
	Leaving behind a lasting legacy for our family
	Spending more time with our family and travelling more
Your Goals and Objectives	To sell our business and be financially independent at age 60/61
	To pay £100k off our mortgage in 2023
	To move to £1m new home in 2024
	To gift house purchase deposits of £50k to our 2 sons in 2035
	To purchase a motor home £50k deposit in 2023
What could stop these plans from being achieved & what are the factors to bear in mind?	Premature Death or Serious Illness
	Business failure
	Economic downturn and fall in investment values, increases in taxation and inflation
	Running out of money by overspending

Recommended Strategy & Actions	***Cashflow Planning / Financial Independence / Pensions***
	Complete a spending plan, and review cashflow model in line with your life events and goals.
	Maximise your pension allowances of £40k each from your business each year in order to reduce corporation tax and diversify your wealth.
	Consolidate your accounts and invest in a portfolio for growth over 10 years
	Taxation
	Discuss options for insurance in trust to cover potential Inheritance Tax using £3k pa annual gift allowance to fund contributions.
	Make use of all tax-free allowances for dividends, interest and maximise your ISAs
	Invest £10k each into a VCT for tax-free growth and to receive £3k each tax rebate
	Liabilities & Debt
	Re-Mortgage to a lower interest rate of 3.5% 5-year fix and increase the monthly payments on your mortgage by £10k pm.
	Risk Management & Asset Protection
	Set up a Legacy Preservation Trust to protect the funds in your pensions
	Increase life and critical illness cover by £500k each now.
	Investment & Portfolios
	Consolidate your investment accounts to simplify tracking and strategy, diversify asset allocation and reduce risk.
	Invest in a portfolio to provide steady growth and beat inflation over 10 years
	Estate Planning & Legacy
	To review and rewrite your Wills. To put in place Lasting Power of Attorney finance and health
	Set up investments for your son's home deposits
	Create a legacy document file and a vision document.
	Hold a family estate planning meeting.

How to get the most value from your financial plan

As I've explained, a financial plan will constantly evolve as you do. This means it's essential to revisit it regularly, at least once a year. However, depending on your circumstances it can be beneficial to assess your financial position more frequently. Business owners, for example, will benefit from carrying out a cash flow modelling exercise every 90 days. This process does more than just give you visibility over your personal and business financial position, it also introduces accountability and will therefore help you avoid procrastination over actions you need to take to improve your financial situation.

Every 90 days, you can create a new to-do list and prioritise it accordingly. Each time you meet with me, we'll work through this list, tick off all the items you've completed and you will visibly see the progress you're making towards your goals. It's incredibly motivating. This is essentially the implementation process for your financial plan, whether you have a business or not. It's about making a list of the things you need to do between your reviews, whether you're having these every 90 days, every six months or every year.

Committing to taking action is the key to getting the most out of your financial plan and the expertise of your financial planner. While I could give you a 50-page financial plan, I know that this will be overwhelming for the vast majority of my clients. Instead, I prefer to give you a one-page action plan that clearly sets out your mission and values, along with the potential obstacles to achieving your goals and what strategies we will use to mitigate risks and help you move towards those goals. This holistic action plan will cover the likes of pensions, investment, life planning and taxation, and contain the actionable steps you need to take to achieve your desired lifestyle.

Getting support with the implementation

When you work through this process of creating your financial plan and regularly checking in on your progress with a financial planner, you get much more than just an action plan and a regular meeting. You will also get access to that financial planner's team who can alleviate some of the work associated with filling in paperwork and contacting your various financial providers. My team will also assess any information you send us to make sure we have what's required to act on your behalf. This makes the whole process of taking action less onerous and much simpler for you.

My aim, and that of everyone on my team, is to make it as simple as possible for each of our clients to implement their financial plans. We also have connections with other professionals, such as lawyers, tax advisers and accountants, with whom we can put you in touch to facilitate the aspects of your financial plan that we are unable to help directly with.

Starting anything is always the hardest part. We all know that if we haven't been for a run for several years, the first time we go out again many of our muscles will ache because they aren't used to working that hard. The more we go running, the easier it becomes. Overcoming the inertia to get up and go for a run is often the most challenging part and it's no different when it comes to overcoming the mental inertia of getting started with your financial planning.

The initial stages of creating your financial plan will, naturally, require the most work. You'll be gathering and providing all the data I talked about in the previous chapter to assess your financial position. However, this is an exercise you only have to do once. Thereafter, it is about making sure you update the information you have shared with your financial planner regularly, rather than having to carry out a detailed fact-finding mission every year.

Once you start on this journey, you will start to tick tasks off your list and with each one you will move one step closer to your desired lifestyle. At the same time, when you work with a financial planner you will have a committed team supporting you and doing some of the heavy lifting. The longer you are on this journey, the more you will see the value in what your financial planner can offer and the more time you will save. However, to reach this point, you have to commit to the process and put in the time. What I can tell you is that, as time goes by, this will become easier and easier.

The key is to be realistic about what you can achieve and for the process of taking action to feel manageable rather than overwhelming. This is why a one-page action plan is so beneficial, because it breaks down what you need to do into achievable steps.

Enjoy the journey

Creating and following your financial plan is all about the journey, not about the destination. In fact, no one wants to reach the destination, even if it's you living to be 100! There is, of course, an inevitability about the destination and my advice is always to enjoy the journey as much as possible.

I want you to arrive in the right place: one that is comfortable for you and your family, happy and secure, and one that you can enjoy as your journey continues. My focus isn't on the destination, it's on helping make your journey as comfortable and enjoyable as possible, whether you're driving down the motorway or taking a more scenic route. Success isn't determined by what you achieve at the end of that road, but about how much enjoyment you get out of the drive itself.

My focus is very much on making sure you can live comfortably and enjoy the life you have now, even if you're working towards building a stronger future, rather than on making considerable sacrifices today on the promise of some golden tomorrow.

A piece of the puzzle

In this chapter I've covered some of the more practical elements of creating and then implementing your financial plan to show you how a financial plan can add real value to your life and not only help you build a stronger future, but also enjoy your life today.

While you may discover you need to make changes to your lifestyle if it is unsustainable, I don't advocate anyone sacrificing their comfort and struggling today for the promise of easier, more comfortable times in the future. I want to help you find the balance between living a comfortable and fulfilling life now, and planning for a financially stable and wealthy future.

Chapter 8
A TALE OF TWO FAMILIES

A tale of two families

Two of the greatest family fortunes in history were created in the 19th century.

One family thrives and prospers to this day.
The other collapsed.

Cornelius Vanderbilt

1794 – 1877

Cornelius Vanderbilt created one of the greatest fortunes in world history valued, at his death, at $100 million. He left 95 per cent of his estate to one son and divided the rest among his eight daughters and his wife, leaving a tiny portion to charity. Four of his children contested the will and one ultimately killed himself over the escalating feud about the financial inheritance.

Economist John Kenneth Galbraith said that the Vanderbilts showed, "both the talent for acquiring money and the dispersing of it in unmatched volume," adding that, "they dispensed their wealth for frequent and unparalleled self-gratification and very often did it with downright stupidity".[15]

Confirmation of that view came only 48 hours after Cornelius' death when one of his direct descendants died penniless. Within 70 years of his passing, the last of the ten great Vanderbilt Fifth Avenue mansions in New York City was torn down.

So great was the destruction of the Vanderbilt family and its wealth that for decades, and through the mid 1900s, the press referred to it as "The Fall of the House of Vanderbilt". William K Vanderbilt, grandson of Cornelius, said of his inheritance, "It has left me with nothing to hope for, with nothing definite to seek or strive for. Inherited wealth is a real handicap to happiness. It is as certain death to ambition as cocaine is to morality."[16]

Cornelius employed a legion of attorneys and accountants. In fact, his planning was based entirely upon financial planning and estate planning. However, he did not consciously prepare his children to receive their inheritances, create a pattern of

---

15   https://www.theheritageinstitute.com/

16   Arthur T. Vanderbilt (2012) *Fortune's Children –The Fall of the House of Vanderbilt,* William Morrow & Company

communication amongst the family, or organise them for on-going success. Consequently, when the Vanderbilt family held a reunion in 1973 there were no millionaires left among them.

Sir Nathan Mayer Rothschild, 1st Baron Rothschild

1840 – 1915

The story of the rise of Europe's Rothschild family in the 19th and 20th centuries is far more than a tale of banking or politics. It is also the story of how one family has intentionally prepared and organised its children to be strong, independent and successful on their own, apart from the family and its vast fortune.

The family first rose to prominence in the late 18th century under Mayer Amschel Rothschild. By the time Sir Nathan Rothschild came to lead the family's enterprises at the turn of the 20th century, the name Rothschild was synonymous with banking and finance. So great was their power that on several occasions the House of Rothschild, as it came to be known, actually bailed Germany and England out of economic catastrophes that could have led to their collapse.

The Rothschild family philosophy on passing inheritances from one generation to the next is very different from Vanderbilt's. They actively mentor their children. For example, they establish "family banks" to lend money to those children who want to start businesses or pursue other careers and they monitor and advise the ventures in which the children participate. At the annual family gatherings (which have been held for over 200 years), the values which have sustained the family for generations are affirmed even as their vision for the future is sharpened and clarified. As part of that vision, the family supports a programme of philanthropy in the arts, medicine, science and education.

The Rothschilds not only utilised financial planning and estate planning, they incorporated legacy planning, which prepares their heirs to receive their inheritance. Building on that very stable platform has been the key to keeping individual family members, and the family as a whole, unified, strong and prosperous for generations, no matter what is happening in the world around them.

"It requires a great deal of boldness and a great deal of caution to make a great fortune.

When you have got it, it requires 10 times more wit to keep it."

Nathan Rothschild[17]

---

17   Bibliographic record: C. N. Douglas (1917), comp. *Forty Thousand Quotations: Prose and Poetical.*

What is legacy?

Legacy is a word that's used in a multitude of contexts. You hear it being talked about in sporting circles, in terms of athletes leaving an "Olympic legacy", for example. You hear it in academic circles, with regard to the legacy of someone's body of work. You hear it in politics, in relation to the legacy a leader leaves for their country. Within financial services and estate planning, "legacy" has traditionally been equated solely to money.

Some people see the word "legacy" in terms of their estate and think of it as money, but as the example from the Rothschild family at the start of this chapter shows, your legacy can be financial, but it can also be social and philanthropic. Another potential misconception around the concept of legacy is that it is always positive. However, this isn't always the case and certainly, when it comes to estate planning, if you haven't prepared correctly your legacy can prove to be more of a burden than a gift to your loved ones. Essentially what I'm talking about is being mindful of what you leave behind, both in terms of your finances and any other areas of your life.

As you can see from the story of the Vanderbilt family, if you don't take steps to protect your legacy within your lifetime, it can easily disappear. In fact, there is data that shows that much of the wealth that someone accumulates in their lifetime has disappeared within three generations. You can spend years building up a business or building your wealth, so you need to consider how to protect that in future generations so that you're not giving up your time and energy to amass this wealth for your family's future only for it to be destroyed within just two or three generations.

Leaving a legacy is about much more than writing a will and creating an estate plan. While both of those are important for passing on your wealth efficiently when you pass away, it is just as important to have a vision for what you want to happen to that wealth once you are gone and to prepare your family for receiving that wealth. This involves sharing your personal wisdom and your vision for your social legacy. All too often, the world prepares the money for families, but it doesn't prepare the families for the money. This is particularly the case for younger members of the family, who may be less experienced at managing money and wealth.

We've all heard stories about people suddenly coming into wealth – whether it's through a lottery win or an inheritance – and these huge sums being squandered. This is a common occurrence when the money has no value beyond the financial. There isn't a story to the wealth that these people want to continue and they don't receive any guidance about how best to use it. The result is that it's too easy to view this money as a windfall or a bonus, which then gets spent as though it's "free", rather than seen as something to preserve for future generations.

For me, legacy is about sharing knowledge and principles, and communicating what needs to happen next to protect that money for future generations, not just the one that immediately follows you.

Why think about your legacy now?

By this point, you have created your financial plan and you've worked out what is going to happen with your money for the rest of your life. The next logical question is what do you want to happen after that, and how long do you want your wealth (and your legacy) to continue for? What do you want your wealth to do, not only for you but also for your family and their future? Once you know how you want to leave a legacy, you also want to consider how you can prepare your family to receive that legacy and what knowledge you can share to help them make good decisions and protect themselves.

Even if you fall into the camp of people who want to leave all their money to a charity, surely leaving a legacy that enables you to keep giving for years or even decades to come is better than making a one-off donation? There are many ways to leave a legacy and a financial planner can help you assess the various options so you can decide which is best for your circumstances and to support the legacy you want to leave.

Begin by identifying the vision for your legacy

There are several stages to thorough legacy planning, but it always begins with identifying your vision. This is similar to what I talked about at the start of this book as the foundation for your financial plan. I want to understand what each of my clients wants, what's important to them and what they want to achieve by leaving a legacy. This involves a certain amount of reflection, and if anyone comes to me who is unsure what their vision for their legacy could be, I will help them uncover that through a series of questions.

In many cases, the people who come to me or Simon for assistance with legacy planning are existing clients and we therefore know them relatively well already, which makes this process easier. If you already know what your core values are, having uncovered these as part of the process of creating a financial plan, this is a good place to start as these often relate to and tie in with the legacy you'd like to leave for your loved ones.

Before having an initial meeting, I ask my clients to fill in three documents about their legacy. The first relates to your financial legacy. This covers your beliefs about money, where they come from, your experiences with money and any financial lessons you'd like to pass on. The second is about your creative vision. This is where you outline your values, what's important to you and the instructions you want to pass on to your family. The third document relates to your personal legacy. Here, you can share the story of the generations of your family who have gone before you. You can write about your grandparents, who they were, how they made their money and what their story is. This can be incredibly valuable to future generations, because many of us don't know our family stories and the struggles they faced in the past, or how they made their fortune.

Together, these three documents provide an excellent starting point for conversations about the legacy you want to leave and the most appropriate way to share that.

Even if you don't have any family or close relatives you want to leave your wealth to, it's still important to consider your legacy. You might be leaving your fortune to charity, but you can still outline how you'd like that money to be used and what activities in particular you'd like it to support to ensure the legacy you're leaving is one that is congruent with your values. You can also ensure that this is much more than a one-off donation if you plan your legacy correctly. In doing so, you're creating social wealth that many others will benefit from.

In some cases, you might start leaving your legacy in your lifetime by setting up charitable trusts to begin distributing and managing your wealth now, rather than waiting until you pass away. This allows you to see some of the impact you have.

Exercise: how to uncover the vision for your legacy

If you aren't sure how to start working out what the vision for your legacy could look like, answering the following questions may help get you started. This process involves identifying both the values that were passed down to you and the values you would like to pass on. Think of this as the emotional inheritance you'll leave for your loved ones.

1. List three of your values which you have lived by
2. What is important/what matters to you in life?
3. What have you learnt that has guided you through life?
4. What does success look like to you?
5. What do you believe about yourself that has helped you become successful?
6. What are the most important lessons you have learnt in life so far?
7. What are the most important lessons you have learnt about money?

8. Are there any other pieces of advice you would want to leave your beneficiaries, apart from what you've included so far?

9. What hopes do you have for the next generation?

10. What would you like your beneficiaries to always remember about you?

Exercise: how to uncover your personal legacy

When it comes to uncovering your personal legacy, Simon and I have a comprehensive list of questions that we work through with each of our clients. Answering the following five questions will be a good starting point if you've never thought about this before.

1. What are the happiest memories from your childhood years?

2. What are your memories of your mother and father?

3. What are your memories of your grandparents?

4. What is the story behind how you met your partner?

5. What family traditions would you like your beneficiaries to keep?

Share your legacy plan

Communication is an absolutely vital step once you've created your legacy plan. I'm talking not only about communicating your wishes and your plans with your family and those who will inherit your wealth, but also communication between your team of advisers and other professionals who help you manage your finances. This might be your accountant, tax adviser and solicitor.

Ideally, you will want all of these professionals, along with your beneficiaries and trustees, to meet so that everyone who is involved in your legacy in any capacity knows one another. This will make it much easier for your family and loved ones to manage your estate when you pass away, which is another element of legacy to consider.

Family meetings are another important step when it comes to legacy planning, particularly when considerable wealth is likely to be left. Having this kind of meeting, where everyone who will benefit from your legacy can not only learn about your plan, but also have a chance to discuss it with you is incredibly valuable. You can explain why you are making certain decisions and why what you've set out is important to you.

This is also a chance to make sure that the next generation feels connected to this wealth and it presents an opportunity to discuss what might be important to them, in terms of issues like climate change. It can facilitate very important conversations, not just about the legacy you're leaving, but also how that's being supported through the financial investments you choose.

When you don't communicate this while you're still alive, you often store up trouble for your family, particularly if what's written in your will is not something one or more family members are happy about. For example, I know of one cancer charity that, like many of them, has a programme that asks people to leave a legacy to them in their will. However, the second-biggest cost of running the charity is paying for lawyers to fight lawsuits from beneficiaries who aren't happy that money has been left to the charity. Now, had they known about the gift to charity in advance and the reason their family member chose to leave it, they may well not contend the gift at all.

Look back at the story I shared at the beginning of this chapter about the Vanderbilts and the Rothschilds – one of the major differences between the way the two approached their legacies is in their communication. Vanderbilt chose not to communicate his wishes with his family, other than in his will, whereas the Rothschild family, to this day, actively discuss legacy and prepare the next generation for receiving the wealth.

Make things easy

Another additional aspect of legacy planning is to make it as easy as possible for your legacy to pass down to the next generation. As much as this relates to having that vision set out and communicating your wishes while you're still alive, this also covers practical matters. It's important to make sure you have all your ducks in a row, so that your affairs are organised efficiently and effectively, making it as little hassle as possible for your beneficiaries when you do pass away.

A financial planner, as well as other professionals you work with such as solicitors and tax advisers, can help you make sure that you have all the practical elements of your legacy organised, in addition to helping you create your plan and communicate it with your loved ones.

Dianne and Lee: untangling the estate

Dianne was the founder and CEO of a successful small business. When she died at the age of 43, her partner, Lee, was understandably grief-stricken. What Lee didn't realise was that the grieving process was just the beginning of his troubles.

While Dianne provided generously for Lee in her will, she had not given him a copy of her will, nor had she shared information about the professional advisers who handled her estate. It took Lee weeks of stressful research to track down this important information.

Dianne could have spared him this stress and anguish if she had prepared and shared a list of her key contacts.[18]

Your legacy is about living life

All too often, conversations about estate planning focus on your death and what happens when you're not here any longer. There are discussions about what you're not going to need and about giving money away after you've died, and the truth is that a lot of people simply aren't comfortable talking about this, either with a professional or their family.

Turning the conversation to legacy is a much more positive way of framing it. You are recognising that you're going to live a long and fruitful life and that, at the end of it, you will have wealth to pass on. I'm not only talking about financial wealth, as I've

---

18   Borislow J.A., Marrama M.A., Scott M.F., (2019), If I Had Only Known: Checklists and Guidance Before and After a Loved One Dies, Strategic Vision Publishing, first edition

explained, but also your wealth of knowledge and experience, that you can pass on to the people you care most about.

What often emerges from the process of legacy planning is a document that you can give to your solicitor to keep with your will that offers guidance and instruction to anyone acting as trustees and to your beneficiaries. This might be half a page long, it might be like a short novel! That really is up to you. While it isn't legally binding, it is incredibly valuable for you, your solicitor and your loved ones. If you are still in the process of writing your will and carrying out your estate planning, this exercise will also give you incredible clarity about what you may need to do on a practical level to ensure your wishes are met.

Legacy is a positive conversation, because you're thinking about how you can ensure your wealth, in every sense, far outlives you. Your legacy is a chance to have an impact and make a positive difference beyond your own existence and to know that, even after you've passed away, you will continue to make a difference. It's very rewarding to know that your story can continue beyond your death.

Wealth and legacy: it's about more than money

If you look at the story of the Vanderbilt and Rothschild families, it's clear to see that legacy is not about the money that either family had. What has made the difference is the nurturing and structured approach the Rothschilds have taken to passing on that money. It's this that has allowed successive generations to continue to build on it.

As you know by now, wealth is about more than money and so too is legacy. You don't have to be megarich to leave a legacy that has an impact after you've gone. You might leave a video for your loved ones that explains your story and your values. Just think about how many billions of digital images there are in the world today. Future generations will have a wealth of digital information available to them that can help them to find out about their ancestors and where they've come from. How can you ensure that this information has meaning for them and adds to their lives?

One of my clients and his dad had gone through their family history for the last century, pulling together a book containing photographs, documents like birth certificates and family stories that can now be passed onto future generations. Everyone has experiences and stories to share, regardless of their financial position, and these are just as important, in terms of your legacy, as any money.

A piece of the puzzle

Legacy planning is an overwhelmingly positive activity to undertake. It is an opportunity to share not only your financial wealth, but also your experience, knowledge and passions with those you care about. When you plan your legacy effectively, starting with your vision, and communicate it clearly you are setting yourself up to have an impact far beyond your years on this planet.

It is all about choice, not only in terms of giving you the choice to determine where and how your wealth should be left and what impact that has, but also giving your beneficiaries the choice to talk to you about those decisions. Regardless of whether or not you have amassed a huge fortune, if you ask anyone whether they'd rather be a Vanderbilt or a Rothschild, I'm pretty sure everyone would choose the latter. Why? Because the Rothschild family created a legacy that still has a positive impact not only on their descendents, but many others in the world, to this day.

Chapter 9

HOW FAR CAN YOU GET ON YOUR OWN?

By this stage in the book, you might be wondering how much of this you could do on your own and whether it's a good idea to even attempt it. There are several strings to this, but broadly speaking, without a financial planner to support and guide you through the process, there are a number of pitfalls you may encounter that can limit or even damage your wealth creation. The following are some of the most common pitfalls to going it alone.

1. Lack of access to the software

The first is a very simple practical issue: access to the kind of modelling software I've talked about already in this book. These products are licensed to financial planners and these licences are not cheap to purchase. In addition, it takes years to learn how to use this software effectively and a financial planner with years of experience will likely make it look very simple. However, be aware that this is not as easy as it may look!

2. Challenge of creating a comprehensive plan

The second relates to the process of creating a plan itself. It takes a great deal of skill and knowledge to know how best to pull together all the information about a person's life and arrange that into a clear roadmap that forms the bedrock of your financial plan. This isn't only about inputting the financial information I have about a client into modelling software, but also using what comes out of this in conjunction with everything I know about their goals and objectives and broader life plans to make sure it all feeds into the plan I create at the end of this process.

3. You don't know what you don't know

It sounds simple, but you don't know what you don't know. A financial planner will have spent years learning about all the concepts and potential solutions available to help their clients and they will use all of this knowledge to help you create a financial plan that sets you on the right path towards achieving your goals.

The danger, when you work through this process on your own, is that you're unaware of all the potential solutions or you simply don't recognise that something you're doing now could be a problem in the future.

In addition, a financial planner will work with a team of specialists in other areas, such as investment managers, who spend their days watching stock market movements and making investment decisions on your behalf, based on their considerable knowledge and experience. These people are able to unpick events and work out how those are going to impact markets or individual shares, rather than succumbing to a knee-jerk reaction.

Look at tech company shares as an example. Google, Facebook, Microsoft, Netflix and Amazon are, broadly speaking, all classed as tech shares. However, they all have completely different business models. Amazon is a distributor, Netflix is a subscription service provider, Google is a facilitator, Microsoft is a subscription-based software provider, and Facebook is a social media company. If one of those businesses runs into difficulty, should you sell your shares in all five just because they are all in the same broad industry group? The answer is of course not and an investment manager will be able to make an informed decision to that effect.

This also highlights a potential issue with having only passively managed funds, which follow an algorithm and therefore don't have that same level of human oversight.

4. Forgetting about the importance of diversification

Diversification not only refers to diversifying across different kinds of financial products (like pensions, ISAs, shares etc) but also about diversifying across industries and markets. This is particularly applicable when we talk about investments in stock markets or individual shares. You want to build a portfolio that protects you from shocks in one major market place, either geographically or, as I discussed above, in terms of an industry.

Diversification is also about having investments that carry different levels of risk, so that you can achieve your goals as efficiently as possible without exposing yourself to too much risk. The idea underpinning portfolio construction is that you invest in different assets and asset classes that won't all be doing well or badly at the same time. This might mean you have money in property as well as in stock markets, or that you spread your stock market investments across different indices. The point is, one product or asset on its own won't serve all your purposes.

Think for a moment about Daly Thompson and Linford Christie, both outstanding athletes. If you wanted someone to run the

200m, Linford Christie would be your pick out of those two any day of the week when he was at his peak. However, you wouldn't ask Linford Christie to also compete in the javelin, the 1,500m and the pole vault. For the decathlon, you would want Daly Thompson all the way. He might not be the fastest 200m runner in the world, but he can deliver consistently good results across all ten disciplines and keep that performance up over the course of three days. When it comes to portfolio management and diversification, you're looking for a Daly Thompson – you want consistency of performance in different areas over increasingly long time periods.

5. Missing pieces

Due to a lack of access to professional modelling tools and the challenges associated with creating a comprehensive financial plan that aligns with your goal, you are very likely to find that you are missing important pieces of your puzzle. As an individual, it is much easier to access DIY planners that can help you forecast one specific element of your finances, such as your pension, but much harder to find software that will also incorporate other aspects of your financial life. That's before you consider the impact of various life events on your finances.

This means that what you're left with is a lot of pieces of the puzzle, some of which will fit together but many that won't, and large gaps with no clear picture of what you're trying to create.

6.   A little knowledge is a dangerous thing

This is a famous saying that I'm sure you've heard before and it's particularly applicable when it comes to finances. Everyone has a mate at the pub who recommends the next "big thing" to invest in, or who has "tips" to help your family avoid paying for the long-term care of elderly relatives. Certainly when it comes to paying for care costs, there is a lot of confusion about the rules and legislation because it can be complex. What you have to remember is that, if there were legitimate ways to sidestep that responsibility, that information would be widely available, it wouldn't be a "secret tip" from a guy at the pub.

There are plenty of examples of families being taken to court by a local authority because they have deliberately tried to hide someone's wealth to avoid paying for their care. Aside from the stress involved, the vast majority of local authorities win their cases. Whether it's a tip to avoid paying for care or the next "big" share, keep the old adage, "If it sounds too good to be true, it probably is" in your mind.

Mind the gap

The gap between what you know and can do yourself, and what is actually possible in your circumstances is the one a financial planner can help you bridge. This will very likely be the first time you've considered planning your financial future in a holistic way, which means you won't know all the questions to ask and you certainly won't have all the solutions readily available (if you did, you wouldn't be reading this book!).

This is where a financial planner comes in. I know what questions I need to ask each client to make sure we explore every possibility. In many cases, I will get my clients to think about events they hadn't even considered before. This all comes as a result of my years of experience working in this field. This is knowledge and awareness you simply can't replicate yourself, even if you have access to professional modelling software.

As you have probably realised by this stage, a lot of the information and data you'll use to create a financial plan is very complex, as is the process of considering different scenarios throughout your lifetime. The skill of a financial planner lies in being able to take what is a complex concept and turn it into a simple representation to give you clarity over the way forward.

As Simon points out, we don't need to know about the inner workings of financial planning to be able to understand the roadmap that comes out at the end. "Think about the London Underground for a moment. The Tube map is iconic but its simplicity understates the complexity of the work that was carried out to create it. Just imagine for a moment the work that must have gone into mapping that out, colour coding all of the lines and making sure the stations were in the right place," he says. "The designer has taken something that's incredibly complex and distilled it into something that's very usable for someone who has no knowledge of the inner workings of the Underground or even the layout of London."

This is precisely what myself, and other financial planners do: we make the complex appear simple. Life is made up of a series of small decisions, some of which can prove very important to your future.

Building a picture of your financial future

While I strongly recommend working with a financial planner to create a holistic and comprehensive financial plan, there are some excellent tools available to help you start to work out your position.

Provest Wealth Management has a useful tool that will allow you to model your own financial future. Visit https://provestwealth. truthaboutmoney.co.uk/ to mock-up your own basic plan or get in touch for support.

Be honest about what you can realistically achieve on your own

Throughout this book, I've shared some questions and exercises you can complete on your own. These are intended to help you start thinking about your future, your values and the lifestyle you would like to lead, as well as to give you a simple starting point for assessing your financial situation.

However, working through these questions and exercises on your own is no substitute for doing it with the support of an experienced financial planner. Of course, you could work with a life coach to understand your goals and objectives, but a life coach is missing vital pieces of your puzzle; namely, how to create a comprehensive plan for achieving those goals and how you can use your finances to help you on this journey.

Think of this another way. If you wanted to build a house, would you go out and do this on your own? More than likely, you would hire an architect, talk to them about your vision for your home and allow them to draw up the detailed plans, which would comply with building regulations and any relevant legislation. Once you have the plans from your architect, unless you're a master builder yourself, you will more than likely hire a builder and tradespeople to bring that plan from your architect into reality. You wouldn't consider trying to build a house by yourself, because you would recognise you didn't have the necessary skills, knowledge or experience to do a good job, and this is a house you want to feel comfortable and confident living in.

Even if you are excellent at drawing and want to have a go at drawing up your own plans for your property rather than using the services of an architect, you have to be mindful of what you don't know. Are you aware of current building regulations? Do you know what legislation is being introduced around sustainability in the built environment? Are you confident the designs you draw up will receive planning permission? An architect will have all this knowledge and will factor this into their plans. You might not even realise that you need to swap a gas boiler for a heat pump due to new regulations being introduced, and why would you if you don't work in this field? No matter how good your plans are, if they don't comply with building regulations and current legislation, you won't receive planning permission.

My point is that you not only need someone who is capable of translating your vision into a plan, but also someone who is aware of all the additional legal and regulatory elements that could impact your project. When you consider financial planning in this way, it is very similar to hiring an architect to design your house and a master builder to do the physical work. These professionals will then bring in other specialists who can help with various aspects of the project, from plumbers and electricians to carpenters and plasterers.

This concept of having a team of specialists, all coordinated by one person who knows what your vision and goals are, is one I'll come back to and explore in greater detail in the final chapter.

Time: the most valuable resource of all

We've all heard the phrase, "Life is short", and it's true. Time is one of your most valuable resources, so my question to anyone considering going down the DIY route is, even if you spend the necessary time learning about financial products and investments, is it worth it? If you're busy running a business, I'm willing to bet you don't have hours to spare each week during which you could be researching pension fund performance or watching the stock markets. You're probably more focused on making sure you not only have time to work on your business, but also to spend time with your loved ones and do the things you enjoy most.

If you decide to manage your finances on your own, you're essentially signing yourself up for a second career. Is that what you really want? You can easily spend hours each week buying and selling shares to maintain your investment portfolio, or even hours just keeping track of your finances once you reach a certain level of wealth. Let's look at this another way: would you want to spend hours learning how to maintain and fix your own car, or would you prefer to take it to a mechanic you trust for its MOT and service each year?

The vast majority of us are very happy to pay a skilled mechanic to service and repair our cars every year, because we don't want to take the time not only to do the work itself, but also to learn how to do it to a high enough standard that we'll be safe on the roads. It's really no different when it comes to managing your finances and creating a financial plan. You could spend hours and hours learning to manage your money and then even more hours actually managing it, or you could significantly reduce the time you commit to it and work with a financial planner, safe in the knowledge they have your best interests at heart and are supporting you as you work towards your goals.

Building a relationship with your financial planner is the key

I've outlined some of the main pitfalls you can fall into if you go down the DIY route. Aside from avoiding those, however, there are some very important benefits to working with a financial planner that can not only positively impact your finances, but also the way you live your life.

One of the most important is how you alter your behaviour. When you commit to building a long-term relationship with a financial planner you are signalling that you want support to improve your behaviour around financial matters, whether that's the accountability to budget and watch your spending or a nudge to save more and to do so regularly.

This relationship needs to be built on trust, because you want to know that you can trust your financial planner (and their wider team, which I'll talk more about in the next chapter) to make decisions on your behalf that will help grow your wealth. As a financial planner, I have a great deal of experience and have seen markets rise and fall.

When you are taking care of your own investments, it can be very easy to panic and sell when you see markets falling. However, the reality is that you need to hold your nerve and simply wait for the market to pick up again. This can be very hard to do when you're surrounded by news headlines talking about market crashes and maybe seeing other investors cashing out.

When you have the counsel of a financial planner, you will find it much easier to remain calm in such situations and to trust the decisions they are making on your behalf.

Just look at what happened during the Covid-19 pandemic, when the markets dropped 30-40 per cent in a very short space of time. As an investor going it alone, with £1 million in a portfolio, it would have been very easy to panic and get out of the market. The trouble is, when you sell at the bottom you will struggle to get back in and in some cases, investors completely lose their bottle and never re-enter the markets having crystallised huge losses.

By contrast, at my firm very few of our clients contacted us during this period worrying about their investments, because not only do they have a plan that they are following, but we have also modelled what would happen to their finances in the event of a significant market crash. This gives them peace of mind about the future and allows them to ride out big falls in the market without panicking.

As a financial planner, it's my job to make sure that my clients don't make the wrong decision, at the wrong time, for the wrong reason. Some of my clients got in touch to ask, "Should I be worried?" but they trusted my advice and stayed the course to see the markets rebound. I make sure I talk to my clients about these kinds of scenarios so that, should they happen, they are prepared and understand how the situation is likely to play out.

This is why working with someone who has an impartial view of your situation and who can advise and guide you to keep you on track is so important. We all have our own perspectives and biases, some of which may not be useful, as I discussed in Chapter 2 when I talked about how your beliefs affect your thinking. By building a relationship with a financial planner, you'll have an experienced and knowledgeable professional on hand who can help you keep any unhelpful biases in check.

Focus on what you do best

If you're an entrepreneur with a successful and thriving business, you are likely already aware of where your talents lie. Broadly speaking, this is making money with your business. As a financial planner, I'm not here to tell you how to do that, because this isn't where you need the support. Making money isn't the challenge, but effectively managing it and making best use of tax regulations and legislation is more difficult and requires a level of knowledge you simply may not possess. This is why working with experienced professionals who have that knowledge can add so much value and allow you to maximise the wealth you create in your business, ensuring you take your share in the most tax-efficient way possible.

A financial planner is there to support your business and help reduce the noise you have to deal with. Our role is to gather all the information that's available, combine that with our knowledge of both financial matters and your situation, and distil this into a narrow range of actions that can facilitate decision making. This allows you to focus on what you do best, which is running and making money from a successful business. It's a partnership.

This is true in my work as a financial planner, too. My passion is to deliver outstanding financial planning for the clients who choose to work with me. The plan itself can be implemented through Provest, or taken to any other provider as my clients can understand where action needs to be taken and what new products or services they need to achieve their ultimate goals.

My role is to help you understand what best aligns with your values and what you want to achieve, but it is the experienced investment managers who physically manage your money and do their best to ensure it performs at the level you require.

Even if you are comfortable with investing and have money in investments at the moment, it's still important to get an external perspective and advice from a financial planner, because you may be taking more risk than you need to with your investments. Conversely, you could be in the situation where simply increasing your level of risk by a small amount will help you achieve the lifestyle you want sooner. The challenge is that you won't know this unless you have gone through the kind of modelling exercise I talked about earlier in the book.

Although there are pension plans that will automatically reduce the level of risk in your portfolio as you move closer to retirement, these are far from perfect or an exact science. Given that the age of retirement is no longer at a fixed point, it's not as simple as just saying you'll transition from high to medium risk after 15 years, then from medium to low risk 10 years later. What if your retirement plans change between the date when you set up your private pension (when you're in your 30s) and when you're actually retiring in your 50s? This is not your area of expertise, and it's also not something that you want to mismanage as it can have a significant impact on your financial position, so consider working with a financial planner to take that pressure off and ensure you have a stronger financial future.

The cost of inaction adds up

While creating a financial plan might seem a little overwhelming when you're at the beginning of the process – especially if you haven't found a financial planner to work with yet – the cost of doing nothing can be substantial. While it's hard to precisely quantify what you lose by failing to take action on your finances, an article for *Fidelity*, in 2021, shared that industry studies estimate professional financial advice can add between 1.5 and 4% to portfolio returns over the long term[19].

A large part of this can be put down to the behavioural side of people's relationships with their financial advisers. As a financial planner, I help people make various informed decisions about their finances. This isn't only about giving them the support to keep their bottle in the face of market falls, but also about encouraging them to adopt behaviours like automating their savings that will have a significant positive benefit on their overall financial position in the years to come.

By failing to make a decision about investing or paying into a pension, and instead keeping your money in cash, you are still making a choice, but one that will negatively impact your financial future. For example, if you have £100,000 and you invest that money with a return of five per cent per year, after ten years your investment will have increased in value to £164,000, net of any charges. If you were to find a financial planner and

---

19   Fidelity, (2021), Why work with a financial advisor?, Fidelity Viewpoints, 11 January, available at: https://www.fidelity.com/viewpoints/investing-ideas/financial-advisor-cost

investment managers able to get you a seven per cent return on that investment, you'll have £200,000 after ten years.

However, if you were to keep your £100,000 in cash and leave it in a savings account with one per cent interest per year (which is generous at the time of writing!) you'll have £110,000 at the end of that ten-year period. That is a very significant difference.

The cost of failing to act was also highlighted in the last chapter when I talked about legacy and shared the contrasting examples of the Vanderbilt and Rothschild families. Vanderbilt chose not to act in terms of arranging his legacy and talking about it with his family and look at the outcome.

I've seen similar situations play out, where the person who has accumulated wealth fails to communicate their values and their vision for the future to the rest of their family. The result is that, often, the wealth they built up is gone within years, and in some cases relationships within the family are also damaged in the process. Talking about what you want your legacy to be and engaging trusted advisers who can help you make decisions in yours and your family's interests can be the difference between your legacy lasting and your wealth being frittered away.

Factoring in the non-financial benefits of financial advice

Taking financial advice and working with a financial planner will do far more for you and your family than simply improve the returns on your investments and savings. As you have hopefully gathered by now, the process I use with my clients and the one I recommend you follow, involves taking a holistic view of your life and planning what you want from life, with money simply a tool to facilitate the lifestyle you desire.

A study conducted by Arunima Himawan for the International Longevity Centre – UK, revealed that there are a number of non-financial benefits to taking advice. The five main benefits reported by the people who participated in the research were:

- Improved financial literacy
- Increased control of their financial future
- Greater reassurance
- A boost in confidence
- Reduced worry, with increased peace of mind and feelings of security.[20]

The question I like to ask is what is the cost of not having those things? This is particularly pertinent when it comes to stress.

20 Arunima Himawan, (2020), Peace of mind: Understanding the non-financial benefits of financial advice, International Longevity Centre UK, November

What is the cost of stress about money in your life? Does it cause arguments? Does it stop you sleeping? What price would you put on your peace of mind? The next point to consider is whether you can achieve that certainty and peace of mind if you plan your finances yourself. I can't unequivocally say "No", but I imagine it would be unlikely that you would achieve the same peace of mind that you get from working with a financial planner by doing everything I've talked about on your own.

As I discussed earlier, you also have to consider the time it will take you to work through this process on your own and whether you will take action if you don't have someone else to be accountable to. To create a comprehensive and holistic financial plan will not only take a great deal of time and effort, it will also take a great deal of self-development. Realistically, if you're busy running a business you're not going to have the time, desire or energy to go it alone.

A piece of the puzzle

While it might be tempting to work through the process of financial planning on your own and to manage your wealth and investments without the support of professionals, in the long run this rarely works out to your benefit. As I've highlighted in this chapter, there are a number of pitfalls that it's very easy to fall into when you opt for the DIY route.

The key is to consider working with a financial planner and other appropriate professionals as an investment in your and your family's future, rather than as a cost. Ultimately, you stand to gain far more than just better financial returns when you consider the peace of mind, greater control and confidence that working with an experienced financial planner offers.

A financial planner can not only provide you with vital pieces of your jigsaw puzzle that connect some of the pieces you've already collected yourself, but as I've explained earlier in the book they can also help you see the whole picture you're trying to piece together.

Chapter 10

FINDING THE RIGHT TEAM/ LOOKING FOR HELP

Now that I've outlined the importance of working with a financial planner, you may be wondering how you go about finding a professional with whom you are comfortable with working and who can help you create a comprehensive financial plan and put all the pieces of your wealth puzzle together. There are several aspects to consider when you're looking for a financial planner to support you. The obvious one that many people jump to is qualifications.

What qualifications should a financial planner have?

There are several qualifications you can achieve as a financial planner in the UK, including becoming a Chartered Financial Planner. One of the best financial planning qualifications is the CERTIFIED FINANCIAL PLANNERTM certification from the Chartered Institute for Securities & Investment (CISI).

The reason I single this qualification out in particular is because it focuses on how you can apply cash flow modelling to creating comprehensive financial plans, rather than simply looking at how to carry out cash flow modelling on its own. This distinction is important, because as I discussed in the previous chapter, cash flow modelling on its own won't help you create a holistic financial plan. In fact, looking at cash flow modelling in isolation puts the focus in the wrong place when you're looking to create real wealth: on your money.

However, while qualifications are important, this overlooks the most essential aspect you need to consider when choosing a financial planner: can you work with them and do you feel comfortable talking to them?

It's *not* about the money

As you know by this stage, real wealth is not about the money you have but about how you can use your money to enable you to live the life you desire. This means that a financial planner who can help you create a holistic financial plan that will provide you with clarity over what your real wealth puzzle looks like won't talk to you about financial products in your initial meeting. In fact, they may not really mention money at all.

Instead they'll have a conversation with you where they seek to understand what's important to you, what you want to achieve, what your hopes and aspirations are and what future you envisage for yourself and your family. When you're looking for a financial planner, remember that this will be a long-term relationship, so you need to be comfortable talking to this person about all of these aspects of your life. Money isn't the starting point of these conversations.

When you pause to think about the topics you'll cover in conversation with your financial planner, you'll likely realise that there are very few other professionals who you will talk to about these kinds of topics in your life. These aren't conversations you'll have with your accountant or your lawyer. This puts your financial planner in a very privileged position and this is why it's so important that you get on with your financial planner and that they get on with you. Your initial meeting with any financial planner should, therefore, centre around whether you can see yourself forming this kind of trusted relationship, because finding the right person to support you on this journey is far more important than the financial products they can offer you.

Ask yourself the following questions when you're meeting financial planners with a view to working with them:

- Can I work with this person?
- Do I trust them?
- Are they highly qualified and experienced?
- Are they the right fit for me?
- Do they understand what I want to achieve?
- Are they talking to me in a way in which I understand?

This last question is more important than you may imagine, because communication is foundational for building relationships and you want to find someone who communicates in a manner that suits you. I carry out exercises with each of my clients to find out how they like to be communicated with and to learn how best to engage with them. This might sound like a small thing, but it makes a significant difference to my relationship with them and to their commitment to the process.

It's not uncommon for a first meeting to cover a client's hopes, aspirations and goals for the future without touching on the financial side of their financial plan. As I explained earlier in the book, understanding what you want to achieve with your money and how you want to use it to create a wealthy future are foundational pieces of your wealth puzzle and I need these before I can help bring further clarity to the picture by looking at the specifics of your financial situation.

There are five foundational pieces of the puzzle that you need to put in place, and that your financial planner will help you put in place. However, they need to be pieced together in the correct order, which is:

1. Values
2. Purpose
3. Goals
4. Legacy
5. Money

It's only when we have clarity about numbers one to four that we can look at your money and see how best to use it to achieve what we've set out in those first four steps.

This is also about the process a financial planner uses to get to know you and to help you build your financial plan. In my view, people who are passionate about delivering client-centred financial services take this approach. Life changes very quickly and events outside of our control can impact us in ways we might not have imagined.

A good financial planner wants to help you plan for the certainty of uncertainty, but to do this effectively they have to understand your values, purpose, goals and the legacy you'd like to leave. Only when they know this can they look at how your financial situation could be affected and, more importantly, how to mitigate that impact to ensure you remain true to the values, purpose, goals and legacy you've set out.

I've talked before about the metaphorical crystal ball I have on my desk and, while I can help you predict the future in some ways, there are never any guarantees. In fact, uncertainty is the only thing you can be certain of. This is why planning for that uncertainty is so powerful, because even when you don't know precisely what will happen, knowing that you have at least considered most of the possibilities will give you peace of mind that your plan can flex and change to accommodate those shifts.

Another important aspect of this is having regular contact and reviews with your financial planner. As I said in Chapter 7, a financial plan is not a document you produce once and then forget about. It will constantly evolve and it's important that both you and your financial planner make time to review and adjust it at least once a year, if not more frequently depending on your personal circumstances. All of these adjustments need to start by meeting your values, then achieving your purpose and goals, and leaving the legacy you want. Money is simply a facilitator for each of those elements of your plan.

Look for knowledge and experience, as well as qualifications

I mentioned some of the financial planning qualifications to look for when you are setting out on your search for a financial planner to support you and help you realise the life you want to live, but in reality it's fair to say that any financial planner you engage will have some form of industry-recognised qualification.

Whether you can get on with that person is a much more important benchmark of whether you will be able to develop a long-term, trusted relationship with them. In addition to this, it's also important to look at a financial planner's experience and knowledge. For example, if you're a business owner, does the financial planner you're talking to have first-hand experience of running their own business? If they run their own firm then the answer to this question will be yes, but if they work for a bank, the answer will be no. You might think that, as long as they can provide solid financial advice for your business, this doesn't matter too much. However, wouldn't you prefer to sit down with a financial planner who is empathetic about the daily challenges of running a business because they have been there too?

All businesses, regardless of industry, face similar challenges around cash flow, HR, marketing and people management and, as a business owner, you have to wear many hats each day. A financial planner with their own business will know this all too well, having done the same thing themselves. This will mean that not only will they be more understanding of your situation, but also they may well see solutions that someone who has never run a business might overlook.

What else can they offer?

A financial planner won't necessarily be an expert in every area of financial management, but it is certainly worth asking whether there are other people on their team with specialist expertise in areas such as later life or legacy planning.

Simon has extensive experience of legacy planning, so I work closely with him when my clients require this kind of specialist advice.

Don't be afraid to ask who else is on their team or what other professionals they work closely with to provide advice in areas that are outside of their immediate expertise but that are still vital for creating a comprehensive and effective financial plan. These are simply other pieces of the puzzle and it's important to remember that one person will be unlikely to have the experience and knowledge to deliver all of them. However, if they are well-connected they can facilitate meetings with experts who fill those gaps, thereby ensuring you gain clarity in every area of your life and that your financial plan is fit for the future.

Think about succession planning too

I'm not talking about succession planning in terms of your wealth, but in relation to who will look after you and your family if your financial planner should become unavailable. This may be because they retire or due to ill health. While it's never nice to think about those worst-case scenarios, it is important to consider them. Remember that you are looking to build a long-term relationship. Therefore, you will want to find a financial planner who has a team around them who can step in and ensure you are still taken care of if they are no longer able to.

It's also important to look at the business itself. If you are engaging a sole-trader financial planner, how will they ensure that you're taken care of once they retire? Who will take on their business, or will they simply close? My business is part of a wider network with billions of client funds under management. Unless something extremely catastrophic happens to the economy, it is fair to say that this business will still be around 100 years from now.

While you may not be around in 100 years, what I've been talking about in this final part of the book is planning for not only your future, but the future of your family who will be here once you've passed away. It's important to consider how your wealth will be managed as part of the legacy you leave and it can be very reassuring to know that there is a large support network of qualified and experienced professionals working alongside and behind the financial planner you decide to work with.

In fact, if potential clients don't ask me about succession planning then I make sure I talk to them about it and explain how this will work at my business during our initial meeting, because I want them to feel comfortable developing a long-term relationship not only with myself, but also my team.

What are other people saying?

If you aren't sure where to start when it comes to finding a financial planner, you can always ask people you know and trust for their recommendations. Many of my clients come to me as referrals from people I've worked with for years, and this is always a good place to start.

You can also look at a financial planner's website to see if they have testimonials or case studies available. As well as demonstrating that this professional has the skills and experience you're looking for, testimonials and case studies can also help you start to work out whether they will be a good fit for you. As you read these, can you identify with the financial planner's clients? Do you feel as though your situations are similar? If so, there is a better chance that this financial planner will be a good fit for you.

You're building a unique professional relationship

As I mentioned earlier in this chapter, there are very few (if any) other professional relationships quite like the one you will develop with your financial planner. You will talk to them about your past, present and future, which puts them in a different role from many of the other financial professionals you will otherwise engage with.

For example, your accountant will only ever be looking back at historical data. Many people trust their accountants implicitly, which is great, but even so your accountant is unlikely to make many suggestions about how to manage your finances in the future beyond the likes of suggesting you go from being self-employed to being incorporated. Their role is to calculate your liabilities and what you owe based on what you have done in the past. Their forecasting of future liabilities is all based on historical data.

By contrast, solicitors don't typically want to know about your past and instead focus very firmly on the present. They also aren't in the business of looking at what might happen tomorrow because that could make them accountable for decisions that you make. This isn't a responsibility the vast majority of solicitors want to take on. There may be a small amount of planning for the future in terms of helping you write documents like a will, but they are unlikely to consider the future beyond legal documents like this.

Other financial professionals, who focus first on your money and the products that you need, whether that's a pension, an ISA or life insurance, will only be dealing with one or maybe a couple of aspects of your financial future. What they lack is oversight of the big picture. They might be working on putting together the bottom left corner of your jigsaw puzzle, but they have no idea what will be created in the top right corner.

A good financial planner will connect all of the pieces and will not only be able to see your bigger picture, but will show it to you too. They will be able to connect all of the other professional advisers in your business and life to make sure that they are all working towards piecing together your wealth puzzle and helping you achieve the life you want.

My job as a financial planner is to explore all the life events each client might experience, model and then plan for those, while taking into account all the aspects of their financial life. It's my role to recognise when something is outside of my wheelhouse and to refer my client to someone who has expertise in the areas I don't.

I am always conscious that, in my role as a financial planner, I deal with all the aspects of someone's life. I want to try to take care of everything, or at the very least to provide support, guidance and signposting when something you need help with falls outside my area of expertise. This is why working with a financial planner is about building a long-term relationship and why it's an ongoing process. This approach to financial planning is designed to span your lifetime and, indeed, beyond. It will help you move forward and get the most out of life and out of your money. You should be able to live your life and plan your legacy in a way that meets your values, and be confident that you've done as well as you could with what you have.

Following the right process

I'm sure you're familiar with the safety briefing on an aircraft, where you're told that in the event of an emergency where you need an oxygen mask, to make sure you put your own mask on before helping others. What I do as a financial planner is follow a similar sort of process. I look at each client's life and their expectations and I will always make sure they are comfortable and achieving what they want to in the present, before looking at the next thing. There is a logical process to the advice I provide and therefore to each client's financial plan.

Much like the example I shared in Chapter 9 about building a house, you have to take the right steps in the right order. If you want to build a house, you don't begin the process by purchasing the bricks, you begin by hiring an architect and finding a suitable piece of land. You explore the dream you have for your home and work out whether it's achievable and feasible. When you know that your dream is both achievable and feasible, you have a solid foundation from which you can move forwards. As you'll have gathered by now, financial planning is no different.

When you are looking for a financial planner, it's therefore important to ask them what process they follow and how they will help you manage life's transitions. There are three things that are guaranteed in life: change, death and taxes. You need to consider all three in relation to your finances and a good financial planner will help you in this respect.

Frank: a sudden change in (good) fortune

When Frank first came to me around four years ago, he was looking for advice about a very specific pension problem he was facing. Of course, I took him through the full financial planning process so that we not only addressed this issue, but also created a holistic financial plan for him and his wife.

About two years later, he became a shareholder in a business and another couple of years on from this, a private equity firm bought the business. This has totally transformed Frank's financial position. He now has choice and financial independence, which he didn't before. Our more recent conversations have been around decisions relating to how he will pass his wealth onto the next generation. He has gone from looking at a retirement age of 65–67 to being in a position to retire at 60. We have revisited his plan, looked at what he wanted to achieve, ticked off what has already been done and have looked at what is left. With this influx of money, many of the things Frank and his wife wanted to do have suddenly become very achievable. Now he's working with Simon to explore his legacy and put a plan in place which fits with his values, purpose and goals.

Encouraging behavioural change

I talked in the first part of the book about behavioural finance and how we all make decisions about our money. My role as a financial planner is to encourage my clients to develop positive financial behaviours, whether that's paying off debt, saving more each month or diversifying their investments and savings to help protect them in the event of economic challenges.

You want to find a financial planner who encourages you to examine your behaviour with money and who will hold you accountable for forming better financial habits. In my view, this is one of the biggest positive impacts I can have on any of my clients.

Always ask a financial planner how often you'll meet, how often you'll review your plan and how they'll ensure you stay on track. Without regular check-ins, not only will your plan become outdated, but it is difficult to get the support you need to change your behaviour around your finances.

Part of this behavioural shift may also involve reframing the value of financial advice and planning. As far as I'm concerned, the products that we utilise to achieve your goals aren't the most important part of the equation. What's important is knowing what your goals are and choosing the right products or funds to help you achieve those. Some people can get overly hung up on the charges and cost of financial advice and products. However, as I explained earlier in this book, the benefits you get from taking financial advice go far beyond the headline returns you generate.

It is easy to understand why you might focus on charges and headline costs for both financial advice and financial products, given that the service can feel very intangible and much of the legislation in the financial world focuses on cost. However, you have to consider whether finding the cheapest option would be your approach in other areas of your life and, if the answer is no, then to consider why you're looking for cheap in relation to your finances. As with everything in life, when you pay a fair rate, you will get a much higher-quality service.

When the service you're paying for can help you live according to your values, realise your purpose, achieve your goals and leave a legacy you're proud of, isn't that one worth paying a little more for than the cheapest option on the market?

The reason I mention this is to help ensure you're asking the right questions of any financial planner you're considering working with and highlight the fact that cost and price isn't everything. Rather than focusing on the figures, focus on the value you're getting out of that service. What price would you put on having financial certainty and peace of mind? I'm pretty confident you'd pay more for that than you will for any good financial planner's services and advice.

A piece of the puzzle

Finding the right financial planner – one who has a strong support network they can introduce you to – is a very important part of your wealth puzzle. In fact, when you find the right person, you'll find that not only do the pieces you already have start to fall into place but also that some of the pieces you are missing appear.

What I've aimed to do in this final chapter is give you an overview of how an experienced financial planner works and therefore the kinds of things to look out for when you are contacting or meeting with such professionals. Always be wary if a financial planner spends more time in their first meeting asking about your money than about your life and goals. Remember that true wealth doesn't lie in the size of your bank balance, but in how fulfilled your life is. Money is simply a tool to enable you to fulfil your purpose, achieve your goals and leave a lasting legacy that is in line with your values.

Conclusion
PIECING IT ALL TOGETHER

As you reach the end of this book, I hope you now have a few more pieces of your own real wealth puzzle, or at the very least have realised that you are missing some pieces (even if you don't know exactly what those are). I cannot stress enough the importance of seeing your bigger picture and knowing what you want your future to look like. When you know this, all the other decisions you need to make around your finances and other areas of your life just fall into place. Money is, after all, merely a tool that you can apply to create the life you desire.

My aim, for all of my clients – and now for you – is to help people live a more fulfilled and value-driven life. I want you to not only enjoy your present, but to know that your future will be just as – if not even more – enjoyable. I also want you to consider how you can pass on your wealth and knowledge to your loved ones, in turn helping the next generation(s) to build fulfilled lives, whatever their version of fulfilled looks like.

Life is not a rehearsal and one thing none of us can buy more of is time. I hope that the time you have spent reading this book has provided you with the tools and the means to make more time in the future for the things that are truly important to you, while deprioritising anything that doesn't give you peace of mind. You have a choice about how you live your life, and that is incredibly empowering. You can use the tools I've shared in this book to help you on your journey, or you may decide you would rather save that time by working with professionals who can help and support you.

The personal approach we take at Provest Wealth Management when planning our clients' financial futures is why the majority of our clients are either referred or come from personal introductions. We believe that, provided we continue to deliver the best possible advice and service, this will continue, as our clients recognise the benefits they have received by working with us and likely have family, friends or colleagues who don't appear to be in a similar position.

I hope you have found reading this book a valuable investment of your time and have been rewarded with some new ideas or insights that you can act upon to improve your own plan, putting more of those pieces of the jigsaw in place and improving your wellbeing in the true sense of the word "wealth". If you think passing this book on to someone else will give them the same opportunity, please feel free to do so.

If you would like to learn more about my and Provest's approach to financial planning and wealth management, please get in touch: paul@provest4wealth.com

You can also download the workbook that accompanies this book, where you will find tools that you can use to support you on your journey towards a truly wealthy and fulfilled life.

SCAN ME

ABOUT THE AUTHOR
AND CONTRIBUTOR

Paul Tracey

Paul Tracey has been involved in the financial services industry since 1989. Following a number of years with Liverpool Victoria and Pearl Assurance he established his own financial advice business in 1996, which he has built purely by referral.

He is passionate about helping all his clients build an effective financial plan, through which they can achieve their own vision of true wealth. As a Chartered Fellow and Certified Financial Planner, Paul has not only helped his many clients to make best use of their financial resources to deliver their plan, but is also an advocate to his peers and served as the regional chairman of the Personal Finance Society (PFS) for three years.

Paul is committed to building long-lasting client relationships based on mutual trust, and is aware that in this ever-changing world he needs to continually develop his own skills and knowledge, as well as those of the team around him.

He is an ardent Aston Villa supporter and has encouraged his wife Liz and their two children to continue the tradition. He is always keen to dance at social events and enjoys music, travel, and meeting people.

Simon Cartmell

Simon joined Provest in 2016 as a Financial Adviser to help provide support for our clients.

He started his career in financial services in 1987 and has amassed considerable expertise advising on financial solutions to both private clients and business owner-managers for their personal and business planning needs. He provides comprehensive financial planning to help them better understand how they can achieve their desired objectives. Simon is committed to building long-lasting client relationships and to ensure his clients better understand the decisions they make. Central to this commitment is the delivery of excellent customer service built on trust and honesty.

Simon regularly helps clients with their estate planning needs and care concerns, as well as providing advice and support to their families and those important to them.

In his spare time, Simon will either be watching his favourite TV shows and films, or planning where he would like to take his next vacation, subject to the approval and acceptance of his family.

Printed in Great Britain
by Amazon